MODERN HINDU REFORMISTS

MARYAM ALIZADEH

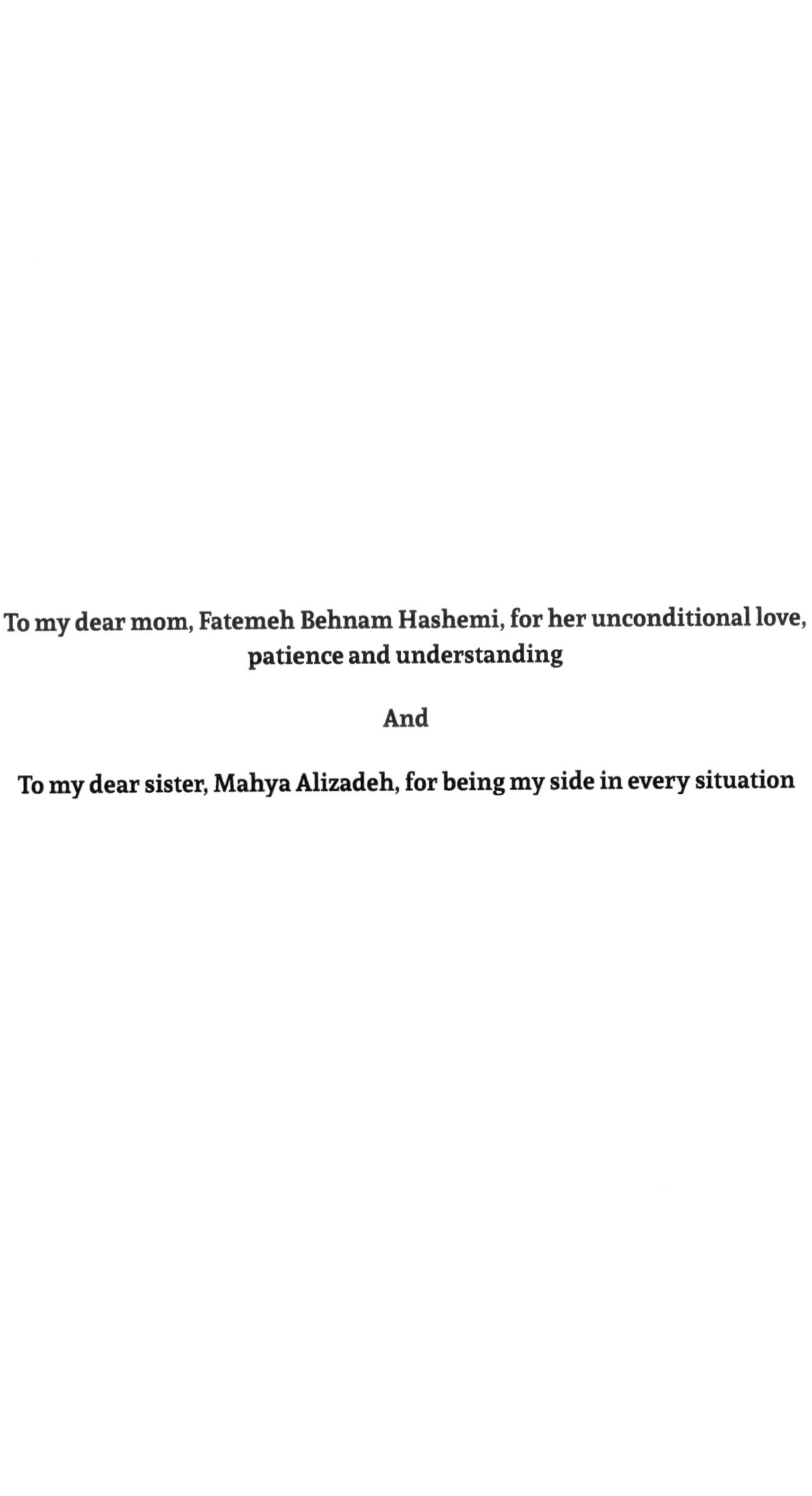

To my dear mom, Fatemeh Behnam Hashemi, for her unconditional love, patience and understanding

And

To my dear sister, Mahya Alizadeh, for being my side in every situation

Contents

Preface

Hinduism is not only a religion but also an Indian socio-cultural lifestyle. After the decline of Hinduism over time, many Hindu scriptures' teachings, such as the Vedas and the Upanishads, were distorted and replaced by superstitions and dogmatic thoughts, the effects of which were visible in society. Hindu socio-religious reform movements in nineteenth-century India played a crucial role in the transformation of Indian society. They tried to reinterpret the scriptures and use the new knowledge to bring about fundamental reform in Hinduism that suited modern life. Also, they could present a new definition of Hinduism to the world. However, there were reasons behind the formation of these movements.

In this book, the author has tried to introduce two Hindu socio-religious reform movements in the nineteenth century to examine the reasons, conditions, and characteristics of the characteristics of Hindu reform movements.

The author has also tried to examine the relationship between Islamic teachings on the formation or reinterpretation of the Indian philosophical and social system by using the case study method on the Ramakrishna and Yogananda movements, in addition to identifying the characteristics of the two.

Acknowledgements

Throughout the writing of this book, I have received a great deal of support and assistance.

I would first like to thank my supervisors, Dr Hamideh Molaei and Dr Alinaqi Baqershahi; their expertise was invaluable in formulating the research questions and methodology. Your insightful feedback pushed me to sharpen my thinking and brought my work to a higher level.

I want to acknowledge Dr Farzaneh Azam Lotfi and Dr Sadrodin Moosavi Jashni, from the University of Tehran, as the second readers of this book, and I am gratefully indebted to them for their precious comments on this book.

I would like to also acknowledge my friend, Dr Arshad Ali Khan, from the University of Jawahar Lal Nehru, for his helpful help and detailed suggestions to improve my research.

In addition, I would like to thank my family for their wise counsel and sympathetic ear. You are always there for me. Thank you.

Maryam Alizadeh

I

About Hinduism

Introduction

India is an ancient civilization and is home to almost one-fifth of the world's total population of 1.3 billion. India is a secular country with no official religion. The diversity of beliefs, languages, and regions in India attracts more attention than in any other country. According to the Ministry of Home Affairs, Government of India, in 2001, the religions in India, in terms of the number of their followers, are as follows: Hinduism (79.8 %), Islam (14.2 %), Christianity (2.3%), Sikhism (1.72 %), Buddhism (0.7 %) and Jainism (0.37 %). The majority of the Indian population follows Hinduism (Ministry of Home Affairs, Government of India, 2001).

According to the above information, most Indians follow Hinduism, but the term Hindu and even Hinduism have a new origin, which means that *Sir Monier-Williams* first used the term Hinduism with the publication of books such as *Hinduism (1877)*. Considering the millennial use of the word Hindu, Hinduism was coined and introduced into Hindi. Early settlers, including Aryans and Greeks, called the inhabitants of India Hindu. Gradually, from the 16th century onwards, the inhabitants of India also distinguished themselves from other tribes by the word Hindu. Nevertheless, this distinction became more religious rather than geographical and cultural. (Doniger et al., 2020). Only groups with distinct non-Hindu identities, such as Jain, Buddhist, Zoroastrians, Muslim, Jewish, and Christian, were not included in the general Hindu category. Ironically, the name later became a general term for all the inhabitants of the Indian subcontinent despite the different religious beliefs of the Indians. Thus, considering most of the local traditions that had grown up in India, Hinduism became a kind of indigenous religious belief for Indians. Indian religions that identified themselves as non-Hindu, such as Buddhism and Jainism, had specific boundaries to distinguish themselves from Hinduism. Still, Hinduism itself never had such boundaries across the subcontinent. The erratic nature of the term Hinduism makes it a fitting title for all the diverse traditions that make up almost eighty percent of Indians and Hindu followers worldwide (Shattuck, 1999).

Religion always has a special place in Indian philosophical, artistic, literary, and social thought history. It can be said that religion is involved in all matters of Indian society and is not like the situation of post-medieval Christianity. There are many reasons for this condition. In India, sacred religious sources such as the *Vedas*, *Upanishads*, and *Gita*, and epics such as the *Mahabharata* and the *Ramayana* were not only Indian religious sources but also sources of intellectual and artistic thought. Moreover, critical philosophical schools such as the *Vedanta* School have been derived from these sources and inspired late Indian thinkers (Parpola, 2015). Whereas in the West, scriptures such as the Bible or the Torah have never been the primary source of inspiration for Western philosophical thought, and Western philosophers, even in the Middle Ages, were influenced by *Plato* and *Aristotle*, not by religion (Majumdar, 1977). During the renaissance, dramatic events took place, and the Western view of science and philosophy changed. Following this change, criticism of the medieval way of thinking began. The situation was gradually prepared for the emergence of humanism, Protestantism, and Secularism movements. These developments resulted in the separation of religion from other spheres of knowledge, after which renaissance thinkers sought to think in a secular or non-Christian context. Such developments have never taken place in India (Farquhar, 1915). As mentioned earlier, Hinduism is divided into Indian traditions and lifestyles, so we cannot separate religion from social structure and norms in India. Religion and the rules of social life in India are not separate, and it can even be said that the two are entirely the same. After the golden age of the Vedas, when The *Brahmins* monopolized Hinduism, distortions were made in it. On the other hand, these distortions were institutionalized in society for hundreds of years because ordinary people were not allowed access to the original texts of the Vedas.

Important periods of Hinduism

For more than two thousand years BC, people lived in the Indian subcontinent with dark skin and curly hair called *Dravidians*, whose descendants now live in the southern subcontinent. The level of Dravidian civilization was equal to that of the *Bronze Age* civilization, and they even had industries and architecture. Recent discoveries at *Harappa* in *Punjab* and the ruins of *Mohenjo-Daro* on the Indus coast have revealed traces of advanced civilization, and it seems that the Harappa-Mohenjo-Daro civilization is associated with *Mesopotamian* civilization. The bridge was on the plateau of Iran. Signs of the religion of these people can be found in primitive religions, such as totems and belief in reincarnation, and traces of its remains are still present among Hindus. Unfortunately, we have not received any written evidence of the religion of the earlier Dravidians (Masson-Ousel, 2013).

Invasion of the Aryans: About two thousand years BC, people called the *Aryans* crossed the *Hindu Kush Mountain range* and came to India. These tribes were tall, white-faced people who called themselves Aryans (nobles). The Aryan tribes were powerful nomadic tribes that came through southern Siberia and present-day Russia to the Iranian plateau to the Indian subcontinent. A group invaded India, invaded the southwest, and conquered the Iranian plateau. For tribes that invaded Iran and India over time, there were changes in their common customs and culture, which in addition to the factor of time and place, marry to natives of these two lands has also been a very influential factor. At the same time, after several thousand years, the roots of both Iran and India are visible in the language and religion (The ancient religion of pre-Islamic Iran). The Aryans gradually settled in India and established villages and towns, turning from shepherds to peasants. They preserved the religious customs of their ancestors in the new land for centuries. Hence, they were polytheists; they made a holy wine called *Soma (Homa)* and offered this drink to their gods (Parpola, 2015).

On the one hand, Aryans were at war with indigenous inhabitants of India, Dravidians, and on the other, Aryans that latter wanted to enter India from other places. The description of these events and wars, which are all epic stories and ancient warfare of the Indian people, is left in books such as *Ramayana* (Ram is the name of a Hindu deity) and *Mahabharata* (the land of Greater India).

After the Aryans conquered the Dravidian natives, they considered themselves a superior ethnic group, the first step toward creating social stratification or caste systems. Besides, the Aryans or the privileged classes were also divided into social categories and tribes. Each tribe had a leader who was called *Raja*. As Raja's power increased, he needed a larger army to protect his borders, thus forming the *Kshatriya* (warlords) class and requiring more clerics to pray for Raja's more significant victories. *Brahman* class was formed.

After establishing the Aryan tribes in the Indian subcontinent and the expansion of the Brahmin caste, myths and oral histories were formed. These stories, which resulted from Brahmanical thought, were originally a collection of recitations and prayers, which they called Veda. The Vedas are the first and oldest sacred books of Hinduism. Also, Vedas are the source of all Indian beliefs, customs and traditions. All laws and regulations have been created within the framework of India's teachings and interpretations and religious rituals, prayers, and social customs. (Frauwallner, 1973)

Hinduism is a collection of countless intertwined beliefs that have emerged and continue to date back to the Vedas. Hinduism has a series of highly diverse beliefs and practices, including the belief in the unity of existence, the originality of unity, the number of goddesses; even monotheism; mysticism, atheism, dualism, and plurality mentioned. A Hindu can be fanatical and careless in religious practices and morals. He may go to the temple regularly and praise the gods, or he may not enter the temple for the rest of his life, and he is also a Hindu. These contradictory matters do not invalidate his Hindu identity. All that is obligatory for him is to observe the rules of the caste system and to believe in reincarnation and rebirth (Zaehner, 2016).

Based on this explanation, we can say about the emergence of Hinduism that this religion is not like other religions formed with the advent of a prophet. Hinduism, in fact, originated from the lifestyle of the people of that time and has gradually reached its present form. Also, according to these explanations, there are important historical points in the history of the formation of Hinduism. Radha Krishnan has divided the philosophical history of India into four main periods, which are 1- Vedic period, 2- Epic period, 3- Sutra period, 4- Scholastic period.

Vedic Period: The Vedic period begins with the invasion of Indo-European tribes and their settlement in the Indian subcontinent. During this period, Aryan civilization and culture developed. This period is the beginning of *Rig Veda* hymns and the formation of Brahmins, and the beginning of the era of the idealism of the *Upanishads*. The oldest surviving works from the Indo-European people are the Rig Veda hymns, which are about praising the gods. The basis of the early thinking of the Indian people is a religion that, in addition to the worship aspect, also had a philosophical meaning that aimed to create unity and connection between the mortal world of man and the infinite world of the gods (Chandra, 1998). The next period is the period of Brahmanism, which coincides with the creation of works called Brahmanas and the period of domination of the Brahmins and priests. During this period, the ritual of worship spread and became the people's beliefs. During this period, the growth of thought did not exceed the limits set by the priests, but gradually with the advent of the Upanishads, which are undoubtedly the most valuable works that Hindu spirituality has presented to the philosophical world, the method of research became esoteric. This tendency to the interior and the search for the inside truth was one of the attributes of the Upanishads. In this way, the Upanishads started to establish a monotheistic religion. This method of Upanishad became the school of Vedanta in the Middle Ages, and its teachings are collected in the treatise *Brahma Sutra*.

Epic period: During the epic period, important events took place in India. The Brahmanical religion, which included the four Vedas and the Brahmanas, took over all religious affairs and reflected its religious organization at the social level as the caste system, thus laying the foundation of a stable organization that dominated all the spiritual affairs of that land. A group of Raja and warriors made changes in the Brahmanical religion by arguing and criticizing it, which led to the creation of Buddhism and Jainism and the worship of *Vasudeva Krishna* (the sect later became the religion of Vaishnavism) and *Pashupati* (this sect later became the religion of Shivaism). However, except for Buddhism and Jainism, these beliefs are reflected in the great epic of the Mahabharata, which represented the time's religious beliefs and is the title of the epic period derived from it. During the epic period, other important works were compiled, such as the *Puranas*, a famous collection of myths. It is also one of the most critical sources of mythological research. In the epic period, the foundations of all Indian philosophical and religious schools were laid, and in the Sutra period, only they became six separate schools (Parpola, 2015).

Sutra period: Sutra refers to the style of writing philosophical principles in the form of terse and concise verses and chapters that express the contents as briefly as possible. By the end of the epic period, the contents of the various philosophical schools had expanded so much that it became necessary somehow to preserve the outlines in the minds of the people and systematize the scattered ideas and opinions. It is tough to know which of these schools was later and which were not. However, the six schools whose works were written in oral form during this period are *Nyaya, Vais'esika, Samkhya, Yoga, Mimamsa* and *Vedanta* (Sullivan, 2001).

Scholastic period: The next period is known as the scholastic period, which begins in the second century AD and lasts until about the fifteenth and sixteenth centuries AD. The tremendous Hindu sages of the period were *Kumarilla, Ramanuja, Vacaspati Misra,* and *Vijnana Behiksu,* and among the Buddhist philosophers were *Nagarjuna, Asvaghosa,* and *Buddhaghosa.* During this period, philosophy became Dialectic, and the method of reasoning was promoted due to these schools' competition. Also, many books and commentaries on the philosophy of Hinduism were written. However, Indian philosophy declined and gradually lost its creative power from the seventeenth century onwards. Subsequent scholars did not add new material to earlier commentators and scholars, but their work in various philosophical fields was less valuable in every way than in the past (Radhakrishnan, 1929).

Almost after the epic period and after the rise of the upper castes of Indian society (around the middle of the tenth century AD), Hinduism lost its dynamism; also, holy books such as the Vedas, Upanishads, and the Gita gave their place to myths and superstitions. Of course, we cannot deny the scientific and philosophical achievements of the Sutra and Scholastic eras. However, the spread of superstition was faster, especially as the upper castes distorted the themes and concepts of the Vedas, Gita, and Upanishad scriptures to gain more power and wealth.

At different times in the Vedas and Upanishads, we sometimes see monotheistic thinking among Hindu beliefs. However, these points are not very strong, and it cannot be said that it is moving towards monotheism. Moreover, for the reasons mentioned, superstitious, false customs and beliefs were gradually institutionalized in people's minds as part of the teachings of Hinduism. In addition to polytheism, we can mention rituals such as Sati, child marriage, Prohibition of remarriage of widows, racism and caste system, untouchability, illiteracy, and belief in magic (Zaehner, 2016).

Apart from polytheism raised in Hinduism, another critical issue that has been reviewed and reinterpreted in each of the reform movements of this religion is the caste system.

Here it is necessary to define the caste system because it was the main reason for establishing many concepts, such as *Sati, Dowry*, prohibition of remarriage of widows and untouchability.

Social class refers to a part of society that differs from other parts of society in terms of shared values, prestige, social activities, wealth, personal belongings, and social etiquette. However, there is another concept called caste, which is opposite to social class. Caste refers to a closed social stratification system where individuals cannot move freely from one social level to another. A person born in a particular caste must spend his whole life in the same caste. Since marriage between different castes is forbidden, there is no way for a person to go beyond his designated caste. Everyone agrees that the class system is better than the caste system. Because in a class system, the transfer of an individual from one class to another is not prevented by government, religion, or culture. Upward mobility, hard work, and marriage to a member of the upper classes are possible in a class system; however, in a caste system, such a thing is impossible (Deshpande, 2010).

Social scientists believe that the word caste's definition is vague and challenging, but they say it is a word with Portuguese roots that have entered the English language. The Anthropological Encyclopedia states that the word may be from Spanish and is probably a derivative of the Latin word for "Castus," meaning chaste, popularized in the mid-15th century by Portuguese travellers entering the Malabar Coast of India. This word apparently means blood and racial origin. The word has even been translated to many categories, queues, or classes. However, all translations show that this word refers more to blood and racial originality and can include chaste, category, queue, and class (Levinson and Ember, 1996).

According to the Encyclopedia of Anthropology, the word caste in Indian society is called *Jaat* or *Jaati*, which means class, category, lineage, generation, and group. *Bottomore*, in his book Sociology, writes of caste: The caste system is unique among social stratification systems. It is not to say that the Indian caste system is not, in principle, comparable to other types of social stratification or that no caste elements are found elsewhere, but that caste systems share a common feature that is related to the division of economic labour in society. It is evident whether we consider natural cast groups (Jati) or four traditional Varnas (Bottomore, 1962). He sees the caste as a closed social group in which marriage is possible only in the form of marriage within the caste. The persons associated with the caste have certain professions, beliefs, customs, rituals, and traditions. No one can go from one caste to another. Humans are born in a caste and remain unchanged in that caste for the rest of their lives. As mentioned earlier, this social class or caste has existed in India since the Vedas and has survived today.

The four main groups of the caste are 1- Brahman (clerics and religious leaders), 2- Kshatriya (military commanders and warriors), 3- Vaishya (merchants and farmers), and 4- *Shudra* (workers). Another group of people do not belong to any of these divisions, which are called untouchable, out of caste or *Dalit*. Each of these castes also has subsets and has its own rules. As mentioned above, mobility between different castes is not allowed, and also, the career among the castes is inherited, which means that the children of a Dalit family must continue the same job as their ancestors (Ghose, 2003).

This system has an interesting point: the famous and spiritual hymn *Purusha Sokta* in Rig Veda's holy book, which means nurture. A well-known hymn formed the basis of the Indian classification system, the caste system. An excerpt from this hymn is as follows:

" When they divided Puruṣa how many portions did they make?

What do they call his mouth, his arms? What do they call his thighs and feet?

The Brahman was his mouth, of both his arms was the Rājanya made.

His thighs became the Vaiśya, from his feet, the Śūdra was produced" (Griffith, 1896).

This hymn later became casts, although there is no mention of inheriting castes. It is important to note that the castes were only about job status. The clergy and the warriors held a higher position than Vaishya and Shudra. However, this position was not hereditary and exclusive. It means that all members of society could be part of the Brahmins and Kshatriyas. Marriage between castes was also possible, and there was no ban on eating food cooked by the Shudras. In other words, there was no sign of the impurity of the Shudra class.

Nevertheless, in the last period of the Vedas, as mentioned earlier, the Brahmins and the Kshatriyas gained greater power and privilege. The privileged power that the lower castes, the Shudra, and the Vaishya, were deprived of those advantages. It was the beginning of caste discrimination. Gradually, the marriage laws with Shudras and touching them were formed during this period because they believed they were polluted.

It can be said that significant changes took place in the caste system and this system's rules during the Smriti period. During this period, Dharma, a set of tasks, became an acceptable process. Smriti set rules for each caste and any relationship in society, including the king and his subjects, husband and wife, teacher and student, etc. These rules were not fixed, and to keep up with new developments, they were sometimes reviewed, and sometimes legislators and clergy expressed their views and imposed bans and taboos. However, since the Gupta Empire, castes and sub-castes have been identified and separated from each other. Relationships between castes regarding wedding parties, touch, and religious rites have been defined. Legal entities such as the *Ganga* (governments), the *Shreni* (guilds and artisans), and the *Sanga* (sects of leaders) that had formed in the early Vedic period disintegrated, and India became a closed and stagnant society. Also, the social status of women was not equal to that of men. For example, widows were not allowed to remarry, women were deprived of their property rights, and Sati (women's self-immolation) was institutionalized.

Why Socio-Religious Movements?

As mentioned earlier, Hinduism is divided into Indian traditions and lifestyles, so we cannot separate religion from social structure and norms in India. Religion and the rules of social life in India are not separate, and it can even be said that the two are entirely the same. For more clarity, we need a few examples here about some social structures that are rooted in religion:

Theory of Caste system: the most important example of this case is the caste system. The caste is a kind of social classification by hereditary transmission of lifestyle, there are many theories on the origin of the caste system, but the famous one says the caste system is of divine origin, based on Purusha Sokta, one of the hymns of Rig Veda's holy book, "When they divided Puruṣa how many portions did they make? What do they call his mouth, his arms? What do they call his thighs and feet? The Brahman was his mouth, of both his arms was the Rājanya made. His thighs became the Vaiśya, from his feet, the Śūdra was produced" (Griffith, 1896). Some Hindu scholars interpreted this hymn for social classifications.

- **Remarriage of widows:** From the ancient tradition of India and the perusal of the scriptures, it becomes clear that widow marriage came in the form of malaise in this society.

There was no prohibition of widow marriage in the Vedic period. Clear examples are found in Rigveda and *Atharvaveda.* For instance: in Atharvaveda, there are some verses about widows' remarriage, such as: "Go up, O woman, to the world of the living; you stand by this deceased one; come! to him who grasps your hand, your second spouse (Didhisu), you have now entered into the relation of wife to husband. (Rig Veda, x.18.8)." Its prohibition is not seen in Ramayana also.

The situation seems to have changed somewhat from the Mahabharata. There are examples of both prohibition and support in the Mahabharata. Also, there are some examples of this prohibition in the Manu smriti, such as: "The marriage-ritual texts are applicable to virgins only, and nowhere among men, to non-virgins; and this because these latter are excluded from religious acts (Manu Smriti, 8.226)." and "Many thousands of unmarried Brāhmaṇa students have gone to heaven, without having perpetuated their race (Manu Smriti, 5.157)" and "Once does the share fall to a man; once is a maiden given away (Manu Smriti, 9.47)".

- **Sati:** One of the claims of the Reformation movements is that Hinduism has been distorted over time, and superstitions have replaced the original teachings of the Vedas. For example, *when we look at the original texts of the Vedas, Sati finds* nothing about Sati and the self-immolation of women. It is even mentioned in the Vedas that widows should be happy. Note this *shloka* (verse) from Rig Veda: "Let these un-widowed dames with noble husbands adorn themselves with fragrant balm and unguent. Decked with fair jewels, tearless, free from sorrow, first let the dames go to where he Lieth (Rigveda, 10.18:7)."

But when we read the scriptures in the post-Vedic period or Atharvaveda (the procedures for everyday life), we see the opposite of what is stated in the Vedas. For example, see the following shlokas:

1. "Choosing her husband's world, O man, this woman lays herself down beside thy lifeless body. Preserving the ancient custom faithfully. Bestow upon her both wealth and offspring (Atharvaveda, 18.3:1)."
2. Although the self-immolation of women is not directly mentioned in Atharvaveda, it is explicitly stated in Purana, another book of Hinduism:

"It is the highest duty of the woman to burn herself after her husband. (Brahma Purana, 80:75)."

3. Another religious text called Daksa Smruti also refers to Sati: "A Sati who dies on the funeral pyre of her husband enjoys eternal bliss in heaven (Daksa Smruti, 4:18-19)."
4. Another reason given to justify Sati in the text of *Kurma Purana* is the forgiveness by Sati of his wife: "A woman who enters the funeral pyre along with her husband shall uplift him even if it is a Brahmana-slayer, an ungrateful fellow or one defiled by great sins. learned men know this to be the greatest expiation for women (Kurma Purana, 2.34:108b-109)."

As we have compared above, after the golden age of the Vedas, when The Brahmins monopolized Hinduism, distortions were made in it. On the other hand, these distortions were institutionalized in society for hundreds of years because ordinary people were not allowed access to the original texts of the Vedas.

Reform Movements: After the invasion of *Mahmud of Ghazni* and the establishment of Muslim rule in India, Hinduism descended into turmoil. The Hindus, on the one hand, lost political power. On the other hand, they faced the dynamic religion of Islam, and gradually a spirit of siege developed among the Hindus. In general, in a period when a nation sees its cultural and religious identity in danger, it turns to prejudice, dogmatism, and the creation of a strict class structure. Dogmatism and imitation are considered a fence to preserve the religion (Richards, 1995). The Hindu community also lost its spirit of religious and philosophical initiative and innovation from the tenth century. Instead of the dynamic ideas of the Upanishads and the Gita, Hindu stories such as the Mahabharata and the Ramayana, which spoke of the past power and glory of Hindu history, became popular. Hinduism's philosophical thought and mysticism gave way to the Brahmins' strict, complex, and simple rituals.

In the social structure of that time, the caste system prevailed. The caste system was, in fact, a Hindu defense maneuver. This system ordered each caste to be careful about its members' behavior and avoid their social relations and marriage with others. If anyone had violated the caste's rules, they would face severe reactions and a social boycott. Like any other nation, the Indians turned to conservatism, rigidity, imitation, and bigotry when they were under attack from stronger cultures and ideologies. Their first concern was to preserve ancient traditions. The Brahmins monopolized the teachings of the religion so that even the Hindus could not directly access their scriptures' contents. The philosophical issues of the *Sutras* also remained a mystery to the people. As a result, ordinary people drowned in polytheism, idolatry, and superstition; then, the tendency towards outward religious ceremonies prevailed (Farquhar, 1915). Women were severely oppressed aside from the caste system and the impurity of a large section of society. *Sati* became such an important religious tradition that the young widows had to sit on the fire with their husbands' bodies and be burned alive. One of the reasons for this custom was a kind of racism and preventing women from converting to Islam and remarrying to Muslim men (Michaels, 2004).

The stagnation of Hinduism was from the tenth century to the first half of the nineteenth century. In this period, there was no news of the dynamic thought of Upanishads and the Gita, but only the prejudice against the names of the Gita and the Vedas increased, and the commitment to their teachings became obsolete. Naturally, in the decline of a society, because no one produces or edits new texts, the old texts become idols and are sanctified. Also, prejudice against old theories increases and is distorted (Farquhar, 1915).

The renaissance of Hinduism began in the nineteenth century. The nineteenth century was when India was entirely under British colonial rule. Interestingly, during this dark period of British colonialism, the movement for self-restoration, the renaissance, and the revival of philosophical, religious thought began in India and flourished in the first half of the twentieth century (Jones, 1989).

From the late 19th century, many Indian scholars started studying ancient India's history, philosophy, science, religions, and literature. This growing knowledge of India's past glory and interaction with the Muslims opened a new path to the Hindu reformers, who presented a new reading of the scripture and Hindu sacred texts regarding personal, social, and spiritual aspects. Therefore, Hindu reformers and revivalists led several new movements to emerge in the Indian socio-religious arena (Farquhar, 1915).

The new interpretation of the sacred texts helped the reformers in their religious and social reform work against all types of inhumane practices, superstitions, polytheism, etc. Since most unjust social practices had become associated with religious beliefs, most social reform movements were religious.

Religious reforms in Hinduism began with prominent Hindu philosophers and scholars. They worked to abolish castes and untouchability, Sati, child marriage, superstition, social inequalities, and illiteracy (Kopf, 2015). In their interpretations, many modern religious reform movements emphasize monotheism, reject idol worshipping, and reject the caste system. The new interpretations are a comparative Islamic approach to God. There is little knowledge of these movements in Iran about Hindu reformist movements. It is assumed that some of these reforms have been influenced by Islam's teachings. For more clarification, we should bring a brief history of the process of these reforms (Jones, 1989).

The initiator of the new renaissance of Hinduism is *Raja Ram Mohan Roy*, one of the Brahmin from Bengal's nobles. *Raja Ram Mohan Roy* started the Reform Movement in 1828, and after him, other leaders, inspired by his actions, continued the reform of Hinduism more widely and comprehensively. If we want to classify Hinduism's reform movements in terms of content and history, they can be divided into four periods:

1. 1800-1828: The period of establishing the foundations of the movement and westernization.
2. 1828-1870: The period of creating a reform movement.
3. 1870-1900: The period of Ideological defense and return to the original teachings of Hinduism.
4. From 1900 onwards: The intellectual, philosophical, and political system and the war period for the independence and maturity of the Hindu political, reformist, and fundamentalist movements (Farquhar, 1915).

During these four periods discussed in chapter 2, many reform movements were formed, some of which were successful and some of which failed. It is impossible to study all these movements in one book; therefore, to answer this question, we will examine two cases of social and religious reform movements in Hinduism in this book. The first is the *Ramakrishna Mission (RKM)*, and the second is *Paramahamsa Yogananda.*

The reason for choosing these two movements can be summarized as follows:

The first selected movement, the Ramakrishna Mission (RKM), can be considered one of Hinduism's most important reform movements. According to the four categories presented above, the Ramakrishna Mission is one of the third wave movements (the period of Ideological defense and return to the original teachings of Hinduism). This movement has been active in all aspects, individually, socially, and spiritually, and has a high share in the reinterpretation of the Vedas and the Gita. The prominent leaders of this movement, *Sri Ramakrishna* and *Swami Vivekananda*, are among the greatest mystics of the contemporary world who prove the theory of unity and equality of all religions (Beckerlegge, 2000). As mentioned, Hinduism was isolated with the advent of Islam, and on the other hand, over the years, due to the monopoly of religious texts by the Brahmins, Hinduism underwent many distortions and superstition. Also, after Britain entered India and tried to propagate Christianity and British culture in India, Hindu thinkers set out to reform Hinduism by reinterpreting sacred texts such as the Vedas and the Gita. Because if these reforms were not done, the Hindu heritage of several thousand years would be lost (Kopf, 2015).

The *Ramakrishna Movement* was one of the most successful reform movements that reinterpreted the sacred texts under modern society and by examining other religions and was able to respond to the criticisms and questions of Western and Eastern thinkers. Religion in India encompasses all aspects of life, including cultural, philosophical, and social aspects. This movement presented a new structure regarding philosophical, mystical, and sociological views by using new interpretations of sacred texts. In addition to the mentioned reasons, the movement has provided social services to reduce poverty and discrimination between social castes, special services for women, and free education for the lower castes in India. The movement has also attracted followers worldwide (Ramakrishna Mission, 2020).

The second case is *Paramahamsa Yogananda*. The most important reason for choosing this person and his movement is that he is new in terms of time and his interpretation of social life. The *Yogananda Movement* occurred chronologically in the twentieth century after the Ramakrishna Movement. According to the four categories presented above, the Yogananda movement is one of the fourth wave movements. When the reformation within Hinduism was over, and Hindu philosophy had a new structure. Yogananda saw his mission in inviting the West to the teachings of Hinduism and yoga. As an educated Hindu, he appeared in the American and European academic communities and proved *Kriya Yoga* using scientific evidence. Eventually, he established more than 500 centers worldwide, mainly in the United States and Europe, teaching Hinduism, yoga, and meditation. In addition to the newness of the Yogananda movement and the focus on inviting the West, another reason for choosing this movement is that Yogananda offers a new perspective on achieving utopia, which is self-awareness. He believes that peace can be achieved through self-awareness. In this way, we can build a better society. (Yogananda, 1952). Apart from the new attitude of Paramahamsa Yogananda, another thing that stands out about his movement is that he has been able to attract more than thousands of people in European countries and the United States.

The author of the present study claims that there is a relationship between the teachings of Islam and selected reform movements. There are some reasons for this claim:

1. One of the golden ages of the Indian empires is the rule of the *Mughals*, the Muslim rulers. Despite policies such as religious freedom, especially during the reign of *Akbar Shah*, it is natural for Muslims to have more opportunities to propagate their religion. As a result, people became acquainted with the dynamic laws of Islam (Richards, 1995).
2. The conditions of society at that time were very unfavorable for the lower castes. The upper castes utterly monopolized power, prosperity, and respect, especially the Brahmins. The *Vaisya*[1] and the *Dalits*[2] preferred to convert to other religions such as *Jainism* and Islam (Deshpande, 2010).
3. According to *Romain Rolland*, Sri Ramakrishna, the leading figure of the Ramakrishna Mission, was a Muslim for a while, and during that period, he could reach a high level of Islamic mysticism. Even in his book, he mentioned that Ramakrishna had followed Islamic rules.
4. Another leader of the Ramakrishna movement, Swami Vivekananda, and his family were also influenced by Islamic teachings. As Rolland acknowledged in his book on Vivekananda, he and his family had good relations with Muslims and even criticized some Hindu laws and traditions or compared Hinduism to Islam (Rolland, 1929).
5. Another reason for proving the influence of Islam on Hindu society is the harsh laws imposed on women, meaning that Hindus enacted laws such as Sati or prohibition of widow remarriage to prevent the spread of Islam. They wanted to prevent the spread of Islam by enacting such laws (Shamsuddin, 2020).

Why Ramakrishna Mission and Paramahansa Yogananda?

- **Ramakrishna Mission**

Ramakrishna Paramahamsa (1834- 86) was a saintly person who sought religious salvation in traditional renunciation, meditation, and devotion *(Bhakti)*. In his search for religious truth or the realization of God, he lived with mystics of other faiths, Muslims and Christians. Again and again, he emphasized that there were many roads to God and salvation and that the service of man was the service of God, for man was the embodiment of God (Mehrotra, 2011).

His great disciple, Swami Vivekananda (1863—1902), popularized his religious message and tried to put it in a form that would suit the needs of contemporary Indian society. Above all, Vivekananda stressed social action. "Knowledge unaccompanied by action in the actual world in which we live was useless." Swami Vivekananda said. Like his guru, he proclaimed the essential oneness of all religions and condemned any narrowness in religious matters. Thus, he wrote in 1898, "For our motherland, a junction of the two great systems, Hinduism and Islam ... is the only hope". To spread his ideas, he established the Ramakrishna Mission in 1897 (Nikhilananda, 1953).

- **Paramahamsa Yogananda**

Paramahamsa Yogananda (1893- 1952) was an Indian monk, yogi, and guru. He spent more than 30 years in the USA. Yogananda was a chief disciple of the Bengali yoga guru *Swami Sri Yukteswar Giri*. He was sent to the West to teach Yoga, show the unity between Eastern and Western religions, and spread Indian spirituality.

Because of his strong influence on the American yoga movement, especially the yoga culture of Los Angles, he was considered the "Father of Yoga in the West."

His "plain living and high thinking" principles attracted people from all backgrounds among his followers; also, in 1952, his organization, *Self-Realization Fellowship (SRF)*, had more than 500 centers in India and the USA (Self-Realization Fellowship, 2020).

Paramahamsa Yogananda has profoundly impacted millions' lives with his comprehensive teachings on the science of Kriya Yoga meditation, the underlying unity of all true religions, the art of balanced health and well-being in body, mind, and soul.

He was the founder of the Self-Realization Fellowship. Also, he taught Kriya Yoga and meditation to many peoples through his organization. (Nelson, 2018)

According to Yogananda-SRF, His teachings and the meditation techniques he taught are available today through:

Self-Realization Fellowship Lessons a comprehensive home-study series originated by Yogananda, Programs conducted by ordained monks and nuns of the Self-Realization Fellowship Monastic Order at SRF temples and meditation centers all over the world, books, recordings, and other publications from SRF, the organization he founded to disseminate his teachings worldwide" (Self-Realization Fellowship, 2020).

[1] The lowest caste among the Hindu caste system

[2] A group of people who are considered as out of the caste and untouchable

II

The Advent of Socio-Religious Movements in India

Before entering the main discussion of this book, namely the two selected movements, it is necessary to explain the reform movement, its characteristics, and its types.

Therefore, this chapter will define the reform movement, its types, and characteristics. Then, in particular, our focus is on socio-religious reform movements.

In addition, we will examine the factors behind the formation of reform movements in India and their specific features. In this chapter, while explaining the intellectual and social characteristics of religious-social reform movements in India, it is tried to introduce the prominent figures of these movements.

Social Movement

A social movement is a form of collective action to transform society or change a part of that society. Social movements have had a significant impact on social change and the history of modern governments since the beginning of the eighteenth century. Sociologists use this concept concerning a group that aims at social change. Social movements are usually formed to distribute power or when decisions that politicians and people take in power have failed to address important current issues and do not meet the needs of the majority of society. Social movements are very similar in appearance to collective actions (Christiansen, 2009). However, there are four significant differences between social movements and collective actions:

1. Temporary collective actions are transient and unstable, with chaos spreading after a flare-up and extinguishing after a few hours or at most a few days. However, social movements are long-lasting.
2. Social actions occur spontaneously, but social movements are determined and purposeful.
3. Collective actions are not coherently structured, but social movements are structured. For example, gathering hundreds of thousands of people for protest demonstrations requires organization.
4. Collective actions involve a small number of people, but social movements affect a large number (Moore, 1978).

The social movement needs an active core. Other people can provide resources such as money or votes to the movement without being too active. In general, they all feel group belonging and strive to achieve a common goal, in other words, when members of the movement come together. Moreover, the spirit and intimacy of a group rule them. They all came to a common belief that what is wrong should be corrected in such a case. According to *Moore*, people are more tolerant of injustice than mobilizing themselves to change it. Feelings of injustice form the basis of social movements, and perceptions of what should be are a license and a sense of duty to break social norms and regulations. It leads to anomalous social behaviors. One of the main goals of social movements is to bring about social change in various ways (Blumer, 1969).

Various classifications of the social movement have been made by sociologists, one of the first classifications being made by *Herbert Blumer*. According to Blumer, social movements can be divided into three categories: 1- General social movements, 2- Specific social movements, and 3- Expressive social movements (Blumer, 1946).

1. General social movements: "Gradual and pervasive changes in people's values – changes which can be called cultural drifts," Blumer said (ibid.: 199-200). According to Blumer, general social movements increase

people's perception of their rights and privileges. These movements do not have specific leadership, are not planned, and do not need a membership. Examples include the women's rights movement and the children's rights movement.

2. Specific social movements: As Blumer points out in his book, specific social movements pursue specific goals. These movements are structured and strive to achieve the goals of an organization. They have a clear membership and accepted leadership, which leads to greater solidarity between members of the movement. Reform and revolutionary movements are examples of this category.
3. Expressive social movements: These types of movements do not seek institutional change in the structure of society but are caused by a kind of pressure and tension. It can be said that this type of movement is formed to express dissatisfaction and may affect the overall personalities of the participants. Religious movements are like this.

Reform Movement and Its Characteristics

Reform movements do not seek to overthrow society and bring about fundamental change but rather to make minor changes in the current state of their community. Reform movements do not deny the norms and values of society but strive to reform and promote them (Williams, 2004).

Characteristics of Reform Movements

- Striving to build a good society is at the core of any reform movement.
- Religious influence: The concept of a good society, apart from its liberal dimension, is often based on religious principles and beliefs. Perhaps for this purpose, Wilkinson (1971) describes reform movements as "emergencies" or "sub-movements" of more significant religious movements. Also, many sociologists and historians believe that the Bhakti movement of medieval India influenced the nineteenth-century movements in India.
- The participation of the educated middle class: The reform movement, as a means of planned and directed changes, often attracts the educated and intelligentsia of the middle class. For example, the leaders and intellectuals of nineteenth-century reform movements in India were people like *Ram Mohan Roy, Ishwar Chandra Vidyasagar, Mahadev Govind*

Ranade, Jyotiba Phule, who were from the educated middle class of India.

History of Hindu Reform Movements in India

In 1757, the British defeated *Siraj al-Dawla,* a Muslim and Shiite ruler of Bengal, in the famous *Battle of Plassey* and established the direct rule of the British company *East India Company* in Bengal. After the defeat of two other powerful Muslim-Shiite rulers, Shuja al-Dawla, the ruler of Oudh in the *Battle of Buxar,* and *Sultan Fatah Ali Tipu,* the leader of Mysore in the late 18th century, British colonial rule spread throughout India. King Gurkani became king of Delhi Castle. He was practically in British captivity, and the prominent ruler of India was the English viceroy based in Calcutta. The *East Asian Company* was a prominent British capitalist company. The primary purpose of the company was to market and plunder India's primary resources. The establishment of political rule or the development of culture and religion was not at the top of their agenda. They exercised political power only to provide economic resources. They even prevented Western missionaries; because they were worried about the revolt of the religious Indians and the jeopardy of their financial interests. Nevertheless, around 1800 the policy of the British company changed, and the cultural-religious invasion of the West began in India. The British rulers, *Lord Clive, Hastings,* and *Cornwallis,* played a significant role in this development (Jones, 1989).

Until the beginning of the nineteenth century, British corporate policy was based on three pillars:

1. They were influencing Hindu sentiments: The British usurped power from the Muslims. Therefore, they could not expect Muslims to cooperate with them. Instead, they pursued a policy of gaining the support of a seventy-five percent Hindu majority and, with the help of Hindus, suppressed *Siraj al-Dawla, Shuja al-Dawla, Haidar Ali, and Tipu.* The East India Company stopped most Christian activity and tried to run Hindu temples. British governors paid Brahmins, and even brutal Hindu rituals, such as Sati and prostitution in temples, were protected by law. The policy of temple management continued even in the first half of the nineteenth century. The last temple was handed over to the Brahmins by the British government in 1862. (Farquhar, 1915)

2. Preventing the development of Christian cultural-religious activities and paying exclusive attention to economic interests: To gain the support of the Hindus, the *Bahadur Company*[1] stopped the activities of the first group of missionaries. *William Carey*, a famous preacher, was forced to settle in the Calcutta area under the pretext of farming. The above policy ended in 1813 after the *Charter Act* of 1813[2]. From then on, the British government explicitly supported the missionaries, and the invasion of cultural colonization began (Richter, 1908).
3. Attention to the Hindu community and their use in the administrative structure: According to conservatism and influence on Hindus, the British government used Hindus in government and administrative employment until 1813. "British policy at the time was such that thousands of new Christians were barred from government employment," says Carey (Richter, 1908: 24). Towards the beginning of the nineteenth century, British policy changed dramatically. Their goal was not just marketing; Rather, it developed India's culture, religion, and political sovereignty. In 1800 *Lord Wellesley* established the *Fort William College* in Calcutta and invited Carey's famous missionary to head and teach there. The British government left the creation of schools to the missionaries.

On the one hand, the cultural-religious invasion and development of missionary activities and, on the other, the development of Western education led to the creation of the Hindu renaissance movement. At the head of the policy of developing the colonial cultural program was Lord Wellesley. After the defeat of Sultan Tipu in 1799, the British government concluded no need for a conservative policy. The battle with Tipu and the fundamentalist development among the Hindus may have compelled them, through the missionaries, to break the religious-cultural resistance of the Eastern nation. Wellesley's brother, later known as the *Duke of Wellington*, defeated *Napoleon*, and the British no longer felt threatened on a global scale. So, the situation was ready for a change in British policy. In 1813, when the sovereignty of the East Asian company was about to end, the British Parliament extended it under certain conditions. Among the conditions was granting greater and complete freedom to Christian missionaries. The missionary attack provoked the reaction of the Hindus (Williams, 2011).

Between 1828 and 1870, the heyday of the Hindu reforms, Christian activity also peaked, and British rule was established throughout India.

After the Indian resistance was crushed in 1857, India became directly part of the British Empire. *Queen Victoria* now ruled India instead of the East India Company. Punjab was the last semi-independent province of India, which was annexed by the British in 1849. After the end of the 1857 uprising, the British government prioritized the reform of Indian society. *William Bentinck*, Queen Victoria's viceroy, initiated the state reform movement. Bentinck acted according to the unique slogan of British cultural colonization, the civilization of the east. Britain's goal is to rule India to improve the situation of the Indians. (Trotter, 1886). At the same time, the British government even interfered in the Hindu religious affairs and, according to a bill, banned the practice of Sati and *Thuggee*[3]. At the same time, the government supported the missionaries' efforts to build new schools. The new educational policy of the government, between 1828 and 1870, created a new class of educated people. Most of them found themselves in management levers, and some were attracted to freelance jobs such as journalism, law, and medicine. Most of the leaders and members of the new religious, social, and political reform movements in India were from the younger generation of Western education (Farquhar, 1915).

Four Periods of Socio-Religious Reform Movements in India

Under these circumstances, a new renaissance of Hinduism began. Raja Ram Mohan Roy, one of the nobles of Brahman Bengal, is the initiator of the new renaissance of Hinduism. Raja Ram Mohan Roy started the reform movement in 1821. The history of India's new movements can be divided into four periods:

1. 1800 to 1828, the period of establishing the foundations of the movement and westernization: It was the height of the invasion of western cultural colonization. Missionaries, orientalists, and some Westerners were at the forefront of the cultural onslaught. Culturally and intellectually, the most prominent figures of this era are Carey and the Serampore missionary group. Serampore Christian Seminary and Fort William College are the mainstays of intellectual activity (Copland, 2006).
2. 1828 to 1870, creating a reform movement: It has been a period of internal reform since 1828. During this period, Hindu intellectuals sought to mobilize internally and reform themselves to eliminate the weaknesses of cultural colonialism to destroy Hinduism and indigenous Indian

culture. This period is a period of laying the groundwork for the defense of Eastern culture and counterattack. Raja Ram Mohan Roy is the founder of the reform movement, and Brahmo Samaj has been the leading religious-social organization of Hindus throughout these forty years. After Raja Ram Mohan Roy, the prolific *Dwarkanath Tagore*[4], *Debendranath Tagore, and Keshab Chandra Sen* are at the head of the Brahmo Samaj movement. At the same time, *Prarthana Samaj*, similar to Brahmo Samaj, was established in Mumbai. A reform movement is also emerging within the Indian Zoroastrians. Indian Muslims engaged in a political fight against the British during this period, culminating in the 1857 nationwide uprising. Some Hindus also took part in this uprising. After the uprising, a group of Muslim intellectuals led by *Syed Ahmad Khan* began an internal reform movement among Muslims. In 1856, *Pandit Ishwar Chandra Vidyasagar* also started a reform movement among the Hindus. His main goal is to protect women's rights, especially Hindu widow remarriage rights. Of course, before Ishwar Chandra's campaign, Raja Ram Mohan Roy had launched a movement against Sati tradition (Kopf, 2015).

3. 1870 to 1900, the period of ideological defense and return to the original Hindu teachings: After the internal reform movement, and the repair of the damage caused by it, the conditions were prepared for the defense of the Hindu religion and culture. The excellent return movement began, and the role of Brahmo Samaj came to an end. In this period, which lasts from 1870 to 1900, Ramakrishna presents the transcendent example of Indian mysticism. *Dayananda Sarasvati* founded the Arya Samaj organization and chanted returning to the Vedas, and Swami Vivekananda rewrote Hindu theology. During this period, the main goal was developing Indian thought in Europe and the United States, for which Vivekananda had prepared the conditions (Jackson, 1994). During this period, the Brahmo Samaj organization declined, and the most important organizations of this period were the Rama Krishna Mission organization founded by Vivekananda and the Arya Samaj organizations founded by *Dayananda Sarasvati*. Among other movements of this period is the intellectual movement of *Shiva Narayana Paramahamsa*. Dayananda Sarasvati, Shiva Narayana Paramahamsa, Vivekananda, and all the prominent figures of the period have rejected polytheism and idolatry, arguing that a return to genuine Hinduism is necessary, leading Dayananda to return to the Vedas; Vivekananda on returning to

Upanishad and Gita; And Shiva Narayana Paramahamsa, on the return to Indian mysticism (Farquhar, 1915).

4. From 1900 onwards, the period of evolution of the philosophical and political system, the struggle for independence, and the growth of reform movements: The fourth period, which begins in 1900 and continues throughout the twentieth century, is the period of systematization. The self-return movement was fruitful, and the West no longer posed a threat to Hindu culture; at this time, the great thinkers began to formulate various philosophical books. The initiator of this phase of Hinduism is Swami Vivekananda. He formulated the new Hinduism as a system. Other contributors to Hinduism include Debendranath Tagore, *Mahatma Gandhi,* and *Radha Krishnan.* At the same time, the flow of specialized academic philosophy was created, and new philosophers created the school of *New Vedantism* or *Realistic Idealism. Hiralal Haldar, G. Subramania Iyer, Ananda Coomaraswamy, Krishna Chandra Bhattacharya* formulated and presented their philosophical system (Beckford, 1986).

Factors behind the Reform Movements of Hinduism

As long as the British pursued a policy of conservatism, the status quo continued, and there was no need to create a new religious movement. Breaking the popular religion was not in Britain's interest; Because they wanted to maintain stability and security. When the British changed their policy in 1800, new schools were created. The primary purpose was to acquaint the Indians with the new culture and civilization of the West. Meanwhile, the missionaries launched a fierce attack on Hinduism. For the first time, young Hindu thinkers became aware of the weaknesses of their religion. The new education opened new horizons for them. These two factors caused them to violate their traditional religion and seek reform. The criticisms and attacks of Christian missionaries in Hinduism and the hate of young Indian scholars from colonization led them to reinterpret and explain it in new ways and defend it. Various theories have been put forward about the factors that led to the renaissance of Hinduism from 1828 onwards. *Farquhar* believes three factors played a vital role in forming Hindu reform movements: the British government, the missionaries, and the orientalists (Farquhar, 1915). The role of the British government in creating reform movements was described in the previous pages. We will now examine the role of missionaries and orientalists.

The Role of Missionaries in India: The history of missionaries in India begins with the Danish missionaries. They entered India in the 18th century and could not carry out evangelistic work due to government restrictions.

As mentioned earlier, the first great preacher in India was an Englishman named Carey. Carey was associated with the *Baptist Church* and entered Calcutta in 1793. He learned Bengali and Sanskrit in Calcutta and translated the Bible into Bengali (Richter, 1908). Raja Ram Mohan Roy helped him in this. In 1800, he chose to work in the Calcutta region, where he established the first significant missionary center and school in India. This center became known as the Serampore School and led missionary activities in the first half of the nineteenth century. Lord Wilsley was asked to take over the management of the Fort William School in Calcutta. He introduced English managers to Bengali and Sanskrit to better manage the natives. This act forced the British rulers not to act as mere merchants but to develop their culture and religion in India.

Apart from Carey, two other missionaries named *Marshman* and *Ward* (Smith, 2011). Serampore missionaries were influential in creating the Hindu reform movement in several ways. Carey was in contact with Raja Ram Mohan Roy, the founder of the Brahmo Samaj organization and the vanguard of the Indian Reform Movement, and Raja Ram Mohan Roy probably borrowed many of his ideas from the Serampore missionaries. Of course, when Ram Mohan published his monotheistic view of the Bible and accused the church of distorting the Bible and the teachings of Christ, the missionaries of Serampore were opposed him (Sharma, (Ed.), 1988). The missionaries of Serampore made notice of Raja Ram Mohan Roy and other teachers in Bengal to the need to abolish the Caste system and Sati. They did this indirectly by attacking Hinduism for having the above elements. The missionaries' criticism was intentional. They wanted to make Hindu youth pessimistic about their religion, but their efforts backfired. Instead of accepting the criticism of Christian missionaries, the educated youth of India decided to reform Hinduism; it was a step towards the beginning of the reform movement of Brahmo Samaj, which later took on the role of the abolition of the missionaries.

The second great Christian missionary in India was named *Alexander Duff*. Duff, in 1830 enters Calcutta. He concluded that Christianity could not be promoted in India without weakening traditional Hindu religious beliefs and drawing them to western culture. To this end, he established an English-language school in the center of Calcutta, which became one of the most important schools. Raja Ram Mohan Roy collaborated with Duff in founding this school. One of the main subjects in this school was teaching the Bible. Duff's activity marked a new stage in the missionaries' efforts.

Since then, missionaries had increasingly established new schools. Bengal youth got to new training turned. Duff was somewhat successful in his goal. The new school's first generation of educated people became Westernized, and some converted to Christianity. Keshab Chandra Sen and his followers, who later openly converted to Christianity, were among them.

At the same time, *Dr. John Wilson* undertook a similar mission in Mumbai with *John Anderson*, another missionary based in Madras. The missionaries spread their network throughout India.

At the same time, nuns and female missionaries became active. They even found their way inside the harems of the kings and made women pessimistic about their religion. They could attract some women to Christianity. However, we can say Christian nuns were not ineffective in creating an awakening among women.

Between 1870 and 1900, the missionaries turned their attention to the Dalits and other backward castes of Hindu society and were more successful. The ninety percent of those in Kerala, Madras, Mizoram, Pandicheria, and others, who converted to Christianity were either the Dalit and *Shudra* castes or primitive tribes living in the mountains (Frykenberg, (Ed.), 2013).

New British Education for Hindus: The development of the Western education network has played a significant role in creating the Hindu renaissance and the reformation movements. Until the early nineteenth century, East India Company officials and colonial planners opposed developing new education among the natives. Farquhar mentioned that many British dignitaries, business people, and capitalists opposed the development of education among the natives. Another British scholar, *Meredith Town*, believed that British efforts to change Hindus' way were futile (Farquhar, 1915).

Around 1800, English planners reconsidered their position. They seem to have concluded that the continuation of colonial rule is possible only when the religious beliefs of the Eastern nations, the Indians, weaken. From then on, the colonizers, with the help of the missionaries, took special care in expanding their educational-cultural system. In this way, they hoped to alienate the Indians from their culture and make them obedient human beings capable of accepting colonialism. Priests such as Duff, Wilson, and Anderson established the first new schools in the major cities of Calcutta, Mumbai, and Madras. Calcutta and Bengal were also education leaders, followed by Mumbai. In addition to the missionaries, some other scientists were involved in developing the new education. Among them was *David Hare*. He established boys' schools in Calcutta. Another English scholar, *Beethoven*, sought to establish girls' schools. In Mumbai, *Elphin Stone* set about developing a new education. As a result of the development of the Western education system, a new group emerged, later called the *Elite Group*. Some educated became the leading supporter of Westernism, as the colonizers expected (Frykenberg, (Ed.), 2013). However, others put the new knowledge and methods in the new schools to serve their religion, for example, *Raja Ram Mohan Roy, Debendranath Tagore, Swami Vivekananda, Brahmananda, Sri Aurobindo, and Mahatma Gandhi.* They became the principal founder of the struggle against the political and cultural colonization of the West and one of the pillars of the return movement. In this way, the development of new education eventually helped the renewal movement (Farquhar, 1915).

Presence of Orientalists in India: Farquhar also considers Orientalists as one of the essential factors in creating the new renaissance of Hinduism. Orientalists were involved in creating a new intellectual-religious and social movement in India in two ways.

First, they removed the sacred religious texts from the monopoly of the Brahmins and, by publishing them, allowed the educated young generation of India to become acquainted with their sacred texts and books directly. Second, they used new methods of critique, research, and interpretation in Hindu religious texts. Their work, though biased, guided the committed educated of India. Indian scholars even used Orientalists' research and method to criticize and refute the positions of Orientalists.

Another point is that their critiques and attacks on Hinduism forced educated youth, such as Ram Mohan Roy, Keshab Chandra Sen, Vivekananda, and Sri Aurobindo, to interpret their religion that Western Orientalists do not attack it. The attacks of orientalists provoked the religious-national prejudice of the Indians (Farquhar, 1915).

Around 1800, Orientalism began in India. The British governor, *Warren Hastings*, opened a school of Indology, Wellesley College, following the British government's new policy to develop cultural colonization. The Fort William School also opened at the same time. There, British administrators learned Sanskrit and Bengali. In 1776, Hindu jurisprudence was translated into English by order of the viceroy, and in 1785, Charles Wilkins translated the Gita into English. At the same time, Sir William Jones compiled the great Sanskrit dictionary. Also, in 1789, he translated the famous play *Kalidas*, called *Shakuntala*, into English. Learning Sanskrit is a turning point in western linguistics. At the same time, the westerners also learned the Pahlavi language. *Anquetil de Peron* went to India. He obtained a copy of the Avesta and published it in the West. He translated *Darashkooh's Persian translation of the Upanishads* into English four years later. Around 1800, Catholic missionary *L'abbé Dubois* published a book on Hindu customs and rituals in English. In 1828 and 1870, Indology reached its peak. It was during this period that *Hodgson* discovered the literature of Buddhism. *Roth* published Vedic literature and history in 1846. Nevertheless, he said *that Max Mueller* left the most considerable effect. During these years, he published all the sacred texts of the east and their translations in fifty volumes, which were published between 1849 and 1875.

Orientalists' books and researches led Indian youth to discover their religious and cultural heritage through the west. They reinterpreted their religion using the approaches of orientalists and the new method. Such orientalists played an essential role in creating the renaissance of Hinduism. Westerners began oriental studies to govern better and colonize India and other Eastern countries, but their works played a significant role in awakening the east (Powell, 2010).

Characteristics and Nature of Social, Cultural and Religious Movements in India

The first question about the characteristics of modern Indian thought is whether the new Indian thought is new or old, is it of a unique eastern nature, or is it a pure adaptation of the west? If it is an eclectic idea, what elements did it adopt from the west and the east's specific elements?

Radha Krishnan says that the new Indian renaissance is partly due to eastern thought's genius and partly to western thought's influence (Radhakrishnan, 1982). The content is eastern content, but its method is adapted from the West. Old facts have been revised and reinterpreted with the help of this method. *Basant Kumar Lal* also believes that India's new thoughts are a mixture of West and East. On the one hand, it wants to preserve the traditional 5,000year-old intellectual heritage; on the other hand, it cannot abandon Western civilization and cultural approaches. Indian thinkers have proposed a new system. Most of the great leaders and thinkers of modern Hinduism were deeply acquainted with Western philosophy and thought. Swami Vivekananda, Sri Aurobindo, Rabindranath Tagore, Radha Krishnan, *Krishna Morti*, and *Rajneesh* are among those who were well acquainted with Western thought and philosophy. Academic philosophers such as *Das Gupta, Bhattacharya*, and Radha Krishnan specialize in Western philosophy. When they returned to their intellectual heritage, they could not escape Western influence. Basant Kumar Lal and *Chatterjee* believe that the new idea is the best example of the combination of West and East. The Indians were among those who, on the one hand, had a rich Eastern philosophical-mystical system; on the other hand, they were directly acquainted with the West and were, therefore, better able than any other nation to offer a fusion of West and east. *Rama Shankar Srivastava* also says: The new intellectual-philosophical movements of India are of a varied nature. In it, the traditional wisdom of the east is blended with the intellectual approaches of the West (Lal, 1978).

One might think that modern Indian thought is eclectic, but there is a subtle difference between eclecticism and composition and synthesis. Eclecticism is the presentation of Western content in the Eastern format, the synthesis and reconstruction of the presentation of Eastern content in new interpretations. Eclecticism is adapting one part of a particular system and another part of another system and linking it. Reconstruction is the hiring of a new method to present its original system. New Indian thinkers, such as Swami Vivekananda, Sri Aurobindo, and Radha Krishnan, synthesized the West and the East to adopt their Eastern intellectual-philosophical system. The West's theories, arguments, proofs, and discoveries that the whole Eastern system was harmoniously adapted or looked at the old truths from new angles. Sometimes they reinterpreted their own religious beliefs with the help of the Western method (Srivastava, 1965).

Some critics have taken a different view, insisting that the new Indian philosophical, religious, and social movement retells old philosophical theories and is not new. Many Westerners think that India lacks a new idea. After the publication of the great work of Max Muller, a collection of sacred texts of the east in fifty volumes, no one in the West dares to say that ancient India did not have a deep philosophy and thought. Basant Kumar Lal has said: A nation that deviates from its intellectual traditions becomes wandering and strange, has no base, and becomes a blind imitator of others (Lal, 1978).

The main axes in the new Indian thought are the unique axes of ancient beliefs, such as *Mukti*[1], *Moksha*[2], *Atman*[3], *Samsara*[4], *Prakriti*[5], *Maya*[6], *Brahman*, *Karma*[7], *Jana*[8], *Yoga*[9], *reincarnation*, etc. Because of the reliance on ancient categories, modernists and Westerners view the thought of the last one hundred and fifty years as interpretive rather than creative. Nevertheless, as Lal has pointed out, any nation's religious and philosophical thought is continuous.

Many of the reforms, changes, and principles of modern Indian thought align with traditional thought. As Srivastava points out, the difference between the new Indian religious and philosophical thought and the old thought is their axes, themes, tendencies, and attitudes (Srivastava, 1965).

Differences between the New and Old Approaches of Indian Philosophy

Below we will look at some of the differences between the new and old approaches defined by *Rama Shanker Srivastava* in his book *Contemporary Indian Philosophy*.

Religion: a mixture of philosophy, theology, and mysticism: One of the features of Indian philosophy (both old and new) and Eastern thought, in general, is that philosophy is based on religion. There is a demarcation between religious, philosophical, and theological metaphysical issues in the West, but there is no such demarcation in the east, especially in India. Religion and mysticism are the foundation of philosophical thought in India. If we separate religion and mysticism from philosophy, there is no such thing as Indian philosophy. For this reason, *Dr. Radha Krishnan*, a great academic philosopher, in his book Contemporary Indian Philosophy alongside expert philosophers such as *Bhattacharya, Das Gupta, Haldar*, and others, the thought of religious and political leaders such as Swami Vivekananda, Sri Aurobindo, Rabindranath Tagore also examines Mahatma Gandhi, Abhedananda, Bhagwan Das and Ranade (Radhakrishnan, 1982).

Rama Krishna Srivastava is one of the leading academic professors of philosophy. He has a book on contemporary Indian philosophy; In this book, the intellectual system of seven thinkers has been studied. Only three people (Bhattacharya, Radha Krishnan, and Iqbal) can be considered expert philosophers. While Tagore, Rama Krishna, Vivekananda, Sri Aurobindo are mystics and theologians, Gandhi and Ranade can be considered ideologies. Basnet Kumar Lal, another professor of philosophy, also published a book entitled Contemporary Indian Philosophy. In addition to academic philosophers such as Iqbal, Radha Krishnan, and Bhattacharya, the thought of Vivekananda, Sri Aurobindo, Tagore, and Mahatma Gandhi was mentioned in his book (Srivastava, 1965).

Radhakrishnanexplains that *Paul Arthur Schilipp*, a professor of American philosophy, says of the difference between Indian and Western philosophy: India did not draw a line between philosophy and religion in the past and today, while rightly or wrongly we do in Western (Radhakrishnan, 1982).

Man is the main subject of Hindu thought: The center of Indian philosophy and mysticism since the Upanishads and the Gita is the man. Indian thought does not begin with the world, history, or even theology; Rather, it starts with the man and ends with man. Moreover, finally, the man reaches *Brahman*[10] from *Atman*[11]. The emphasis of all old and new thinkers, from the *Rishi* of Upanishads and the Gita to Ramakrishna, *Sai Baba*, Vivekananda, Radha Krishnan, and *Osho Rajneesh*, is that man is a more profound and more mysterious being than we imagine. According to the Western worldview, man is the essence of physical and biological evolution and the master of the world. According to the Hindu worldview, man is God. Man is still at the center of Indian philosophical, mystical, and religious thought. The difference between ancient Hindu thought and modern Hindu thought is a modification of old Idealism and pure spiritualism. In the past, the divine element of man was emphasized, and the physical aspect and needs of man were denied. It is now approaching the Islamic view, which can be called realistic Idealism. According to this view, the essence of human existence is divine, but man is a combination of materiality and spirituality. In this view, man's material needs are not denied. Man is a material and spiritual being.

Cultivating physical strength and spiritual austerity is not considered worthless, which is the big difference between old and new Hindu thought. Islamic influences may also contribute to such a transformation. Still, the main factor in transforming thought from pure Idealism to Realistic Idealism was the influence of the new Western thought. Radha Krishnan, Srivastava, Sri Aurobindo, and others recognized the difference between ancient and modern thought. Srivastava believed that one of the commonalities of the new intellectual-philosophical movements is the recognition of the originality of both soul and matter (Srivastava, 1965). Also, Basant Kumar Lal said India's new thought seeks to reconcile spirituality with materialism. The soul is the essence of human existence, but it is impossible to pay attention to the soul without paying attention to the body (Lal, 1978).

Theory of the evolution of the soul: One of the other differences between ancient and modern Indian thought is the soul's evolution. In ancient thought, Atman was a complete concept without the need for change, and it can be said that the concept of man was separate from it. In the old Indian theory of Atman, there was no evolution. In the nineteenth century, the theory and the common intellectual category became the subject of evolution. Since then, Indian thinkers have introduced the category of evolution into Indian philosophy, and Yoga and Tantra[12] are known as methods for the evolution of the soul (Srivastava, 1965). The new theory is almost similar to the *theory of Substantive Motion* that *Mulla Sadra* states in Islamic philosophy (Tabatabai, 2010).

Realistic Idealism as a worldview: The traditional Hindu worldview is purely idealistic. In this theory, what is true is the essence of Brahman (absolute spiritual existence), and the universe is Maya, deception, and illusion. For example, we dream what we see as reality, and when we wake up, we realize that whatever it was, it was just an illusion and deception. Also, life after death is like waking up. Because the material dimension is deception, there is a contradiction between the material and spiritual dimensions, which is the truth. We must deny matter and body and material and physical needs in order to attain knowledge and salvation. Because material life and the world are worthless, worldly and social activities are also worthless and useless. The traditional view of Indian thought has been quite idealistic. However, the new perspective also values the material world.

Since Raja Ram Mohan Roy, Indian thinkers such as Vivekananda, Aurobindo, Tagore, Krishna Morti, Radha Krishnan, and others have reinterpreted the Maya theory. According to their studies, the originality and value of the matter, the world, the material dimension, and man's material needs should not be ignored. They consider soul and matter together. According to Dr. Haldar, new perspectives can be considered realistic Idealism (Haldar, 2018). The above view is not dissimilar to the Islamic position in this regard. Sri Aurobindo says: The soul and matter manifest truth (Brahman); Matter manifests the lower truth, and the soul is the higher manifestation of the truth. There is no contradiction between matter and spirit; The manifestations of a single truth are on two different levels; these are two different states and levels of manifestation of truth; we cannot say one is right and another is wrong (Radhakrishnan, 1940).

The above explanation is different from the general practice of ancient Indian thought; New thinkers, however, obtain scattered verses from the Vedas, Upanishads, and Gita and interpret them to confirm the new realist theory; But this is just a personal interpretation. In ancient Hindu philosophy, the soul had originality, and the matter had no originality. In modern philosophy, both have originality, and accepting one does not mean denying the other. New Indian thought seeks to reconcile the soul with the matter. The ultimate value is with the soul, but the matter is undeniable. Thus, the new Indian philosophy is not purely idealistic (Srivastava, 1965).

Attention to society instead of individualism: Indian thought in the past was individualistic. The priority of the previous schools was individual salvation and not the well-being of society. The focus of the Yoga, Tantra, and *Bhakti*[13] schools were on personal salvation. In the nineteenth century, following the reform movements in India, a transformation took place, and society and social life emerged as independent objective units. New movements, such as Brahmo Samaj,

Arya Samaj, Ramakrishna Mission, and others, called for improving conditions and creating social justice. Contemporary thinkers consider the reform of society as a necessary condition for saving the individual. Sri Aurobindo and Radha Krishnan believe that salvation is possible when the world is spiritual. Man cannot attain salvation unless Prakriti becomes *Para Prakriti*[14] (Radhakrishnan, 1982). Srivastava says that in the minds of the ancients, the emphasis is on the resurrection (Srivastava, 1965). Salvation is an individual matter and means releasing the individual from the cycle of birth (in the theory of reincarnation). There has been a change in the thought of modern philosophers, still talking about Moksha and Mukti. However, the main goal is not just to get out of the birth cycle; Man, even after salvation, does not consider finished; Rather, he returns to the scene of existence to save society and other human beings. He will not rest until everyone is saved. The issue of social reform was not discussed in the theories of the ancient philosophers. The philosophical systems of *Shankara*[15], *Nyaya*[16], *Mimamsa*[17] , and *Advaita*[18] believed that salvation is possible even in a corrupt society. Vivekananda and Sri Aurobindo, and others do not accept the old ideas (Aurobindo, 1999).

In the old theory of Hinduism, only the individual was mentioned, and society had no place, and there was no specific law to save the individual. If we want to compare this issue briefly with Islam, we must say that in Islam, the issue of the *Ummah* (people) is raised, and the Qur'an has provided rules for the people of society. According to the Qur'an, Muslim thinkers, especially *Ibn Khaldun*, developed sociology and attributed originality and personality to society independently. Society comprises individuals, but it has an independent nature, identity, laws, and destiny. In the nineteenth century, *Marx*, *Kent*, and then *Durkheim*, *Weber*, *Pareto*, and others developed a new sociological science that emphasized the originality of society. In this atmosphere, a new Hindu intellectual renaissance began. It was natural for new movements to place great emphasis on the social dimension.

Most modern Indian thinkers, like Islamic thought, regard both the individual and society as genuine. Contrary to old Hinduism thinkers, which considered only the individual to be original, and the sociology of Marx, Kent, and Durkheim, which regarded as an only society to be original. The difference between Islamic sociology and other theories is that it does not consider the individual separate from society, gives identity to society, and has birth, decline, and growth. Individuals make up society, then society builds individuals; For this reason, the happiness and salvation of individuals depend on the happiness and salvation of society (Shilling and Mellor, 2011).

As *Motahari* says: The verses of the Qur'an confirm the same theory. On the one hand, the Qur'an believes in the originality of the individual; also, it believes in individual salvation. On the other hand, it provides the rules, suggestions, and system of individual worship for it. In this view, Individuals have the will and authority and are responsible and accountable for their decisions, while the Qur'an considers nations to have a common destiny and common laws. Social life is not an allegory; it is a fact (Abutalebi, 2013).

New Indian thinkers have precisely the same view. Islam or Islam and the West may have influenced the evolution of modern Indian thought.

Global attitude instead of closed attitude: Hindu society is a closed society and has a closed class system (Caste system) in which not only class mobility was impossible, but its cultural connection was strictly controlled. For the Vedas, Upanishads, *Puranas*[19], the world is India, and the only civilization, culture, and religion is Hinduism. Unlike the Greeks or the Muslims, and the Europeans who had information about other religions and nations, the Indians did not know the world outside India. Even after the advent of Islam, only in the group of Hindu mystics and scholars such as Kabir Das and Chaitanya, the adaptation or combination of Hinduism and Islam was raised. Most rural Hindus and Brahmins thought that the only religion in the world was *Sanatana Dharma*[20]. It is true that the mystical-philosophical idea of Hinduism, which was based on the unity of existence, recognized different ways to reach God, and the idea of the unity of religions can be seen even in ancient texts such as the Upanishads, the Gita, etc. They meant the union of different religions only within Hinduism or the branching religions of Hinduism such as Buddhism and Jainism. Kabir Das considered this principle to include Islam as well (Shah, 2008).

From the nineteenth century, a new trend emerged. Most great thinkers, such as Raja Ram Mohan Roy, Keshab Chandra Sen, Debendranath Tagore, Vivekananda, Ramakrishna, Bhagwan Das, and others, have cited the theory of religious unity as one of the fundamental principles of the new approach. Since then, most yogis, such as Sai Baba, and Tantirks, such as Rajneesh, believe that their system goes beyond the limits of Hinduism and that followers of all religions of the world can turn to Yoga or Tantra. The idea of the unity of religions and the worldview are the hallmarks of modern Indian thought. Only the Arya Samaj movement and Hindu fundamentalism are opposed to it. They believe in the principle of religious propaganda, the conversion of religion, and the supremacy of Hinduism as the only true religion globally.

The first movement to gain a global perspective was the Brahmo Samaj movement. Brahmo Samaj emerged in the West-East connection and this atmosphere of elite rule, and it sought to reconcile Hinduism, Islam, and Christianity (Kopf, 2015).

Srivastava, as well as Radha Krishnan, point to this feature of the new thought. Srivastava says Hinduism because it was based on the mystical view of existential unity, already tended to recognize originality in different ways to reach God (Srivastava, 1965). In the middle ages, bigotry, stagnation, and social classification limited Hinduism. In the nineteenth century, reformist movements revived the spirit of tolerance of other religions in Hinduism.

Srivastava considers Ramakrishna to be the most excellent defender of the originality of all religions. It is said that Brahmo Samaj, who was acquainted with Christianity and influenced by Islam, proposed the idea of religious unity to create understanding between the three religions. Then Ramakrishna, who had a mystical view and believed that human beings could reach God in various ways, explicitly stated: All religions are original. His teachings influenced the leader of Brahmo Samaj, Keshab Chandra Sen (Mehrotra, 2011).

Radha Krishnan, Frequiher, and Basnet Kumar Lal also regard tolerance as a feature of modern Indian thought. In mystical thought and specialized philosophical thought, tolerance is a principle. Among the other new elements in line with the unity of religions is the global attitude seen in the new schools. In the past, Indian philosophy was person-centered. The new reform movements of India have de-individualized, and now their goal is not only to save their society but to save the whole of humanity. The view was considered only in Islam, but it was unknown in the old Hindu culture. Some believe that the Hindu community, which is discussed in Arya Samaj and then in the RSS, was adopted by Muslims from Hindus. In any case, the emergence of a global and transnational attitude is a new approach and cannot be found in ancient texts (Srivastava, 1965). Thus, one of the features of India's new approach is the transformation from ethnocentrism to humanity.

Emphasis on the reality of Hinduism instead of complicated and incorrect religious rites: After the Upanishads and the Gita, Hinduism was petrified, and instead of Vedanta mysticism and philosophy, the Brahmins emphasized the practice of complex and challenging Vedic rites. Instead of focusing on the spirit of religion, Hinduism focused only on religious ceremonies. In addition, the telling of the myths and religious stories of *Ram and Krishna* was standard. After Raja Ram Mohan Roy, all the thinkers of the Hindu reform movements emphasized that the essence of Hinduism is not the performance of rituals and ceremonies. Raja Ram Mohan Roy, Debendranath Tagore, Keshab Chandra Sen, Ramakrishna, Vivekananda, Dayananda Saraswati, Sai Baba, Radha Krishnan, Sri Aurobindo all emphasized the reality and spirit of the Hindu religion (Srivastava, 1965).

Returning to the sacred texts of the Vedas, Upanishads, and the Gita: One of the most important slogans of the reform movements in India was the return to the original religion and the teachings of the Vedas, Upanishads, and Gita.

Leaders and thinkers of the Hindu reformation movement felt that one of the reasons for the decline of Hinduism was forgetting the original teachings of the religion and the departure from the original sacred texts. Brahmo Samaj and its leaders, such as Raja Ram Mohan Ray, Debendranath Tagore and Keshab Chandra Sen, Arya Samaj and its leader Dayananda Saraswati, Ramakrishna Mission and its leader Vivekananda, Sri Aurobindo, Gandhi, all believed in returning to the originality of Hinduism (Frauwallner, 1973).

Ram Mohan Roy, Dayananda Saraswati, and Vivekanand asserted that Hindu society in the Middle Ages had strayed from the truths of the sacred texts of the Vedas, Upanishads, and Gita; The Vedas, Upanishads, and Gita were either abandoned or interpreted only by the Brahmins and theologians of the Shankara, Ramanuja, and Madhwa schools (Farquhar, 1915). According to modern thinkers, the only way to revive Hinduism and the dynamism of Hindu society was to abolish the monopoly on the use of the original texts by the Brahmins and the direct reading of the sacred texts by all people. Of course, each reform movement emphasized the revival of different scriptures; for example, Raja Ram Mohan Roy, Brahmo Samaj, Vivekananda, and Rama Krishna Mission, sought to revive the original texts of the Upanishads and the Gita. Krishna Morti and Radha Krishnan also consider Upanishad the most bottomless sacred text and chant the revival of Vedanta philosophy. Dayananda Saraswati and Aria Samaj chant the slogan of returning to the Vedas; Sri Aurobindo relies on Veda and Gita; Mystics and yogis emphasize the Gita (Jones, 1989).

Emphasis on monotheism and rejection of polytheism: The traditional religion of the Hindus was highly polytheistic. In Hindu mythology, the number of gods is so great that the population of the gods is more than the population of the people of India. Even every family had particular family gods (Chandra, 1998).

One of the characteristics of the new religious and social reform movements in India is the rejection or new interpretation of polytheism and the tendency towards monotheism. Raja Ram Mohan Roy started the religious reform movement by attacking Hindu polytheism and idolatry. In this case, the Hindu reform movement is undoubtedly influenced by Islamic teachings. During his studies, Raja Ram Mohan Roy, who was thoroughly acquainted with Islamic texts and culture, rejected idolatry and polytheism under the influence of Islam. Islam was more decisive than the influence of Christianity and the West because Raja Ram Mohan Roy even rejected Christianity because of the *Trinity* and polytheism. He believed that the original teachings of Christ and the Bible were different from what the church says (Kopf, 2015). Debendranath Tagore, Keshab Chandra Sen, and the Brahmo Samaj movement, in general, reject polytheism. Swami Dayananda Saraswati and his organization, Arya Samaj, were strongly opposed to Islam. However, he was consciously influenced by Islamic monotheism through Brahmo Samaj. Arya Samaj also interpreted the Vedas to turn polytheism into monotheism and interpreted the 33 God of Vedas as a symbol of the forces of nature. To this day, the followers of Arya Samaj are monotheists and reject polytheism. Ramakrishna and Swami Vivekananda accepted Hindu gods and pagan rites but justified and interpreted them so that polytheism became monotheism. From the time of Ramakrishna and Vivekananda, the new Hindu idea emerged from monotheism to unity. The old idea of Upanishad was also mystical and existential unity (Farquhar, 1915). Vivekananda, Sri Aurobindo, and Radha Krishnan considered the theory of the unity of existence to be pure monotheism. Radha Krishnan mentioned in his book that the belief in the independent existence of creatures, limiting the nature of God, is also a form of polytheism. Henceforth, the new idea of India is not based on polytheism or theological monotheism but on the unity of existence and mystical monotheism (Radhakrishnan, 1940).

Conclusion of Chapter

What was examined in this chapter was mainly about the characteristics of the Hindu socio-religious movements in the nineteenth century. There were religious movements before the nineteenth century, but the features that make the nineteenth-century movements unique are in fact modernity, attention to the social aspects of religion, and reinterpretation of Hindu scriptures by Hindu intellectuals and scholars. In addition, in this phase of the Reformation, the Reformers emphasize interaction with other religions and seek to lift Hinduism out of isolation, and introduce it as a universal and rich religion.

[1] Freedom from rebirths, Salvation

[2] According to Britannica " Moksha, also spelled mokṣa, also called mukti, in Indian philosophy and religion, liberation from the cycle of death and rebirth (samsara)."

[3] According to Britannica " Atman, (Sanskrit: “self,” “breath”) one of the most basic concepts in Hinduism, the universal self, identical with the eternal core of the personality that after death either transmigrates to a new life or attains release (moksha) from the bonds of existence."

[4] The cycle of death and rebirth to which life in the material world is bound.

[5] Material nature

[6] Magic or illusion

[7] According to Britannica " Karma, Sanskrit karman (“act”), Pali kamma, in Indian religion and philosophy, the universal causal law by which good or bad actions determine the future modes of an individual’s existence."

[8] Knowledge

[9] According to Britannica "Yoga, (Sanskrit: “Yoking” or “Union”) one of the six systems (darshans) of Indian philosophy. Its influence has been widespread among many other schools of Indian thought. Its basic text is the Yoga-sutras by Patanjali (c. 2nd century BCE or 5th century CE)."

[10] According to Britanica, Brahman is the Supreme Entity described in the Upanishads. It is the Brahman that is said to manifest itself into this universe.

[11] According to Britanica, Atman, one of the most basic concepts in Hinduism, the universal self, identical with the eternal core of the personality that after death either transmigrates to a new life or attains release from the bonds of existence.

[12] Liberation of energy and expansion of consciousness

[13] According to Britannica "Bhakti, (Sanskrit: “devotion”) in Hinduism, a movement emphasizing the mutual intense emotional attachment and love of a devotee toward a personal god and of the god for the devotee."

[14] The upper nature

[15] According to Britannica "Shankara, also called Shankaracharya, philosopher and theologian, most renowned exponent of the Advaita Vedanta school of philosophy, from whose doctrines the main currents of modern Indian thought are derived. He wrote commentaries on the Brahma-sutra, the principal Upanishads, and the Bhagavadgita, affirming his belief in one eternal unchanging reality (brahman) and the illusion of plurality and differentiation."

[16] Justice, a philosophical school in Hinduism

[17] Reflection, a philosophical school in Hinduism

[18] According to Britannica "Advaita, one of the most influential schools of Vedanta, which is one of the six orthodox philosophical systems (darshans) of Indian philosophy."

[19] According to Britannica "Purana, (Sanskrit: “Ancient”) in the sacred literature of Hinduism, any of a number of popular encyclopedic collections of myth, legend, and genealogy, varying greatly as to date and origin."

[20] Hinduism

[1] East India Company

[2] According to the Charter Act 1813, which was approved by the United Kingdom Parliament, the rule of the East India Company over India was extended. The charter also allowed Christian missionaries to preach Christianity.

[3] Thugee means the murder and robbery of travelers, was popular in the northern parts of the Indian subcontinent and particularly India.

[4] Father of Debendranath Tagore

III

Ramakrishna Mission (RKM)

As noted in previous chapters, throughout India's several thousand-year histories, many personalities have worked to improve the social situation and revive the religious attitude of the people of this land. Some of these reform movements led to an independent religion in the early centuries, including Jainism, Buddhism, and Sikhism. Indeed, social affairs could be a severe factor for religious movements (Jones, 1989). However, the Indian youth put Western knowledge at the service of their religion and reconsidered their religion in the face of the West. In the meantime, the Ramakrishna Reform Movement was formed. Ramakrishna and Vivekananda founded Neo-Hinduism by creating religious and social changes (Farquhar, 1915). In the nineteenth century, various religious movements emerged in India, the Ramakrishna Reform Movement being one of the most important. It was influenced by other cultures and, based on the common elements of religions, tried to quickly update itself according to the needs of today's world (Jackson, 1994).

By explaining the two theories of monotheism and existential unity, Ramakrishna not only gained the experiences of mystical life but was also able to reinterpret the aspects of the religious-social life of the people based on the belief in the harmony of religions and monotheism. After him, his disciples collected his ideas about theology, man, the world, and society (Mehrotra, 2011).

The study of the ideas of the Ramakrishna Reform Movement led to the emergence of new theories in India to introduce neo-Hinduism to the world with the integration of other religions. Although this movement introduced new attitudes in Hinduism, it still considers itself faithful to the religious traditions of the past (Beckerlegge, 2000). Ramakrishna's spirituality attracted many to him, and among his extraordinary disciples was Vivekananda, who later became known as a controversial spiritual follower and teacher. Also, he founded Ramakrishna Mission (RKM).

The main question of this chapter of the present study: what are the main reforms introduced by the Ramakrishna Mission? Moreover, what are the relationship between the Ramakrishna Mission and the teachings of Islam?

For this reason, it is necessary to provide information about the principal founders of this movement. Therefore, in this chapter, we will first introduce Ramakrishna's character, the process of mystical growth of him, his religious and social attitudes, and his disciples, then introduce Swami Vivekananda and the Ramakrishna Mission and finally examine the similarities between Islamic teachings and the principles of the Ramakrishna Mission.

Sri Ramakrishna

Ramakrishna was born in 1836. His real name is *Gadadhar Chattopadhyaya*, who later became known as Ramakrishna after reaching high mystical levels.

Ramakrishna was born in the village of Kamapukar in the Calcutta region. Bengal and Calcutta were among the first manifestations of the influence of Western civilization in India and the birthplace of the renaissance of Hinduism. Kamapukar, because it was far from the railway, had no contact with the new civilization and had preserved the old way and tradition. The villagers were very religious and interested in Hindu mysticism. They were also very bigoted about the caste system (Gupta, 1983).

Vivekananda and other disciples of Ramakrishna have mentioned many miracles and extraordinary events about him from childhood to the end of his life (Gupta, 1983). In all cultures, it is challenging to study the life events of mystics; because mythology is so mixed with facts that it is complicated to discern the truth.

However, to be fair in research, the researcher must judge impartially. In addition, from a socio-religious point of view, more significant than how religious leaders live is how their followers think about them. That is why neutral scholars, such as Max Muller, Romain Rolland, and others, have mentioned the miracles that fans attribute to Ramakrishna. Saying these miracles is not as confirming it. These miracles may not be true, or maybe they are myths, but it is vital for the sociologist who works on religions to know what myths a movement is based on and what ideas people are attracted to it (Rolland, 1929).

Ramakrishna's disciples say that his parents had strange dreams on the eve of his birth, including that Ramakrishna's father had a dream that a great mystic, who is the incarnation of *Vishnu,* descends into his house (Gupta, 1983).

Also, Ramakrishna lived in a religious atmosphere. Bengal had a rich Bhakti culture. *Sri Chaitanya,* one of the most famous movement figures, appeared in Bengal. The hymns of Chaitanya and *Kabir Das,* which were based on the sanctification of Vishnu and the goddess *Kali,* were very popular in Bengal (Sadananda, 1975).

It can be said that the first influences in the development of Ramakrishna's character were the influence of poems about gods, including poems of Chaitanya and Kabir Das and *Chandidas* (Isherwood, 1965).

Chaitanya lived between 1489 and 1533. He is the most famous mystic and reformer of the religion of Bengal. He was born in a village where he studied religious sciences and became one of the scholars. Nevertheless, in his youth, he left the seminary and traveled to different parts of Bengal. He sang passionately religious poems and hymns that impressed the people. Hindus and Muslims all were joined him. He promoted the school of mysticism and devotion and advocated the harmony of religions (Saradananda, 2020).

According to Chaitanya, Islam and Hinduism are two ways to achieve the same goal, and like Kabir Das, Chaitanya was influenced by the teachings of Islam (Rolland, 1929). After Chaitanya, a series of other mystic poets emerged in Bengal. Chandidas was one of the most famous. The religious songs of the above poets played a significant role in developing Ramakrishna's thoughts and personality (Saradananda, 2020).

Dakshineswar is a temple in Bengal that marked a new stage in Ramakrishna's life. The temple was built by a woman named *Rani Rashmoni* from the Shudra caste, who dedicated it to worship the goddess

Kali. Also, because Rani Rashmoni respected all religions, rooms were built in the temple for Muslims and other religions to rest. Nevertheless, the problem with this temple was that no Brahman worked as a cleric because they believed that this temple was built by an untouchable[1] (Isherwood, 1965). On the other hand, the Ramakrishna family, who were in financial poverty after the death of their father, decided to work as Brahmin in this temple, and this was a new beginning for Ramakrishna (Gupta, 1983).

Hindus believe that their gods should be treated like humans, preparing clothes and food for the gods and cleaning them every day. In Dakshineswar, these tasks were assigned to Ramakrishna; Gradually, Ramakrishna considered and worshiped the goddess Kali as his mother. Since his childhood, he had experienced many mystical states, but in Dakshineswar, these mystical states increased, and he reached Bhakti. According to Romain Rolland, if this child were in Western society, he would be called a psychic definitely. However, this was not the case in Hindu mystical society (Rolland, 1929).

The process of mystical growth of Ramakrishna

Indian mysticism offers three ways of salvation: The Bhakti method or the way of devotion; The Tantra method or drowning in lust, power, and pleasure; the Yoga method or suppressing instincts and gaining consciousness (D'Souza, 2001).

In Indian philosophy and mysticism, the Bhakti way is based on devotion, the Tantra way is based on gaining power, and the yoga way is based on consciousness. Bhakti is the attainment of salvation through devotion, Tantra is the attainment of salvation through lust and power, and Yoga is the attainment of salvation through Austerity; Bhakti is the religion of the heart, Tantra is the religion of instincts, and Yoga is the religion of the soul and the intellect. The purpose and destination of all three methods are the same; Finding "Self" and attaining "God." The ultimate truth is *Shuddh*[2], *Chit*[3], *and Anand*[4], and there is nothing but these three attributes (Radhakrishnan, 1929).

Indian mysticism has collected three methods to achieve the above goals: Bhakti, Tantra, and Yoga. The above methods are not the initiative of the Hindu mind, but all the valid religions of the world have elements of the above three methods. Nevertheless, the achievement of Indian mysticism codified the austerity methods and formulated them in Yoga, Tantra, and

Bhakti (D'Souza, 2001).

Bhakti: In Sanskrit, Bhakt means devotion, love, affection, worship, faith, and sincerity. Bhakti also means devotion and is part of a religious hymn. *Bhakt* is someone who follows the path of Bhakti. Worshiper, devotee, and lover are among the meanings of Bhakt (Macdonell, 2004). In the terminology of this religion, God or any holy essence that is loved and devoted is called *Bhagavad*. Bhagavad means sacred, pure, divine, heavenly, honorable, and respectable (Macdonell, 2004). The word Bhagavad is also used for the saints of God. Hence the Gita is called Bhagavad Gita. Buddhists have also added the word Bhagavad to their scriptures.

The word Bhagavad is commonly used to refer to the cult of Krishna (Macdonell, 2004). The word Bhagavan (God) is from the same root. In modern Hindi, the word Bhagavan is used as the equivalent of the word God. In Hindi, the most common words for God are *Bhagavan, Ashur, Paramatman, Parmeshwar* (Singh, 1982). Hindus have compiled the Bhakti school in thousands of pages. In it, the philosophy of Bhakti, the method of devotion, states, authorities, qualities of a Bhakti are described in detail. (Doniger, 2018)

In Hindu religious texts, Bhakti is sincere worship and intense devotion to God, or the divine saints. Usually, Bhakti begins with devotion to one of the gods or other holy essences such as *Ram, Krishna, Kali, Hanuman*, etc. In this way, the worshiper reaches the essence of God from the manifestations of God (Davis, 2014).

Bhakti has two stages: Apara Bhakti and Para Bhakti; Apara Bhakti is the love of one of the sacred essences while performing worldly activities; this is the most straightforward way to achieve spiritual pleasure without giving up the pursuit of livelihood and worldly affairs. Para Bhakti is the pure love of God for which man leaves the material interests (Kalupahana, 1972).

The texts of Bhagavad Gita suggest 19 ways for Bhakti, which includes the following qualities:

Love to God as our owner and us as His servants.

Considering God as parents and considering ourselves as children

Considering God as a beloved person and considering ourselves as a loving woman

Considering God as a beautiful woman and considering ourselves as a loving man

Considering God as the owner and considering ourselves as an animal like a dog or a monkey (Movahed, 2019)

Some of the above seem disgusting to those with a monotheistic view, such as considering God as a child or beloved. Such ideas are the result of the primitive and polytheistic thinking of ancient India. Perhaps the *Rishis*[5] attempted to attribute any interest and attachment that a seeker may have to someone to God so that there is no one other than God in his heart (Movahed, 2019).

In Indian mysticism, the intuitive experience of the personal God is obtained through Bhakti and Tantra. Indian mysticism believes that no one can reach this stage without the guidance of a perfect guide, but Ramakrishna reached the stage of intuition without the help of a master (Farquhar, 1977). Ramakrishna experienced other pristine states in addition to the nineteen states mentioned in the Bhagavad Gita. For example, when he saw a Muslim cleric in Dakshineswar, he asked him to learn Islamic mysticism. For this reason, he behaved like a Muslim for a while (Gupta, 1983).

"Ramakrishna converted to Islam for a time and became a Muslim openly," says Farquhar (1977). Romain Roland narrates the story: Ramakrishna asked a Muslim cleric to teach him Islamic mysticism. The name of this cleric was *Govinda Roy*. Apparently, he was a Hindu who converted to Islam. Govinda Roy explained that a Muslim could not worship idols or live in a temple where idolatry occurred. Ramakrishna left idolatry and also left the Kali temple and lived in a cemetery for some time. He dressed as a Muslim and even ate beef, which is a great sin for Hindus. So, while he experienced Islamic mysticism and practiced austerity, he claimed to have seen God and thus reached the highest levels of Islamic mysticism (Rolland, 1929).

Tantra: In Sanskrit, "Tan" means the sound of music, and "Tant" means mysterious, mystical. Tantra is a mysterious method or austerity associated with the sounds of mysterious music. In ancient times, magic was mainly associated with music (Macdonell, 2004). The person who uses the tantra method is called Tantric (Macdonell, 2004).

There are two types of Tantra: *Mantramarga* and *Atimarga*. Mantramarga is, in fact, the same black magic that is prevalent in the world and is familiar to all. In this method, Tantric reaches a limited power by using magic.

Atimarga is a way to reach God by satisfying instincts as a kind of austerity (Mishra, 1981).

Yoga is based on Suppressing and denying instincts, and Tantra is based on saturating instincts. The goal of both is the same, reaching to God.

Indian mystics have divided people into three categories:

1. Those who have an animal nature and tend to have sexual pleasures.
2. Those who have a heroic nature and tend to power.
3. Those who have spiritual nature and tend to be spiritual.

Austerity yoga is suitable for the third category, while the Tantra method is suitable for the other two categories (Avalon, 1914).

Tantra is based on the principle of *Catharsis*. The term Catharsis is used by Aristotle and means to increase pain for treatment. According to this theory, pain leads to treatment when added appropriately (Mishra, 1981). Through saturation, Tantra saves man from instincts and changes his way of thinking. In the Tantra method, power and woman are of particular importance. According to Tantra philosophy, humans have an animal or heroic nature. The woman is the ultimate goal for the animal category, and for the heroic category, power is the ultimate goal. Tantra sees the two as a means to an end. The method of Tantra austerity begins with performing magical acts and worshiping women (Mishra, 1981).

Until 1858, Ramakrishna practiced mystical conduct without a mentor's guidance and mainly used the Bhakti method (Mehrotra, 2011).

In Dakshineswar lived a woman who was a Tantra master named *Bhairavi Brahmani*. She accepted Ramakrishna as her friend and child. It is said: The first question that Ramakrishna asked Bhairavi was: Dear mother! People say I am crazy. Tell me the truth? Bhairavi said: My son, the people of the world are all sinners, some are inclined towards women, and some are inclined towards power and wealth; while you are mad at God, among the multitude of madmen, you are the only wise. Where everyone is mad, the wise are called mad (Isherwood, 1965).

Ramakrishna practiced Tantra austerity under Bhairavi Brahmani. Shortly afterward, Bhairavi realized that Ramakrishna had attained high ranks in Tantra, which were very difficult for others to reach, even for herself. So Bhairavi told everyone that Ramakrishna was not an ordinary cleric but an incarnation of Vishnu. Also, she decided to become a disciple of Ramakrishna (Rolland, 1929).

Yoga: Yoga in Sanskrit means unity. Another meaning of the word yoga is functional performance and performance of duty. Other lexical meanings of the word Yoga, wearing armor and war clothing to protect against enemy attack, healing, method, means, spell, magic, supernatural means, a trick of war, achievement, wealth, property, opportunity, alliance, in It is a combination of different elements. Thus, we see that literally, the word yoga has different meanings. Yoga means a particular system of austerity to create a concentration of thought, improve living conditions and reach God (Macdonell, 2004).

One of the great thinkers and mystics of ancient India, *Patanjali*, collected the system of Yoga. The purpose of this system was to unite the body with the mind, the mind with the soul, and the soul with the general spirit of the world and the essence of God (White, 2019).

A yogi practices austerity in Yoga. Patanjali compilated the yoga system around the 4th century AD. His book, *Yoga Sutra*, is still one of the primary texts of Yoga. Patanjali is not the creator of Yoga. It seems that Indian mystics and Rishis have gradually invented and applied mystical and spiritual austerity methods from ancient times. Patanjali summarized these methods. Two thousand years later, mystics made Yoga the exact and complete science of physical, mental, and spiritual austerity (White, 2019).

At the beginning of his book, Patanjali introduces Yoga as controlling the waves of thought in the mind and the concentration of the senses. Practicing mindfulness is the first step in practicing Yoga. When the ability to concentrate on thought is created, dispersion disappears, and the human mind reaches the facts. "By creating the ability to concentrate, a person can find oneself," says Patanjali. To receive oneself is to receive the essence of God in oneself. "This knowledge is the means of salvation." The concentration of thought distinguishes right from wrong and puts man in complete control. The condition for success is continuous austerity. The element of extreme austerity is vital in the yoga system. Another pillar of the yoga system is suppressing lusts and avoiding any belonging to whatever but Atman. It is an essential element of Yoga (Jha, 2003).

So, since Patanjali, Yoga has been divided into several categories:

Karma Yoga is the path of service through selfless action for the good of others.

Bhakti Yoga cultivates the expression and love of the Divine through devotional rituals.

Jnana Yoga is the path of intellect and wisdom, and its components include studying sacred texts, intellectual debates, philosophical discussion, and introspection.

Raja Yoga, also known as the royal path, refers to the journey toward personal enlightenment. This path balances the three main yoga types described - Karma, Bhakti, and Jnana - while integrating the eight limbs, or stages, of Yoga (Malhotra, 2017)

Eventually, after three years of practicing Tantra, Ramakrishna met *Totapuri*, a great yogi. As soon as Ramakrishna and Totapuri met, they became very interested in each other. Totapuri asked Ramakrishna to follow Yoga to reach Atman. Ramakrishna accepted. After a while, he reached the highest levels of *Samadhi* (Rolland, 1929). It is the highest state of Yoga that itself has some levels. Samadhi is total self-collectedness, or ecstasy, the highest state of mental concentration that people can achieve while still bound to the body and unites them with the highest reality. According to Patanjali's Yoga Sutras, Samadhi is the eighth and final step on the path of Yoga (White, 2019).

Religious Attitude of Ramakrishna

Rama Krishna's religious attitude can be summed up in two ways: 1- Harmony of religions 2- Unity of existence

Harmony of religions: In *Nirvikalpa Samadhi*[6], Ramakrishna understood the principle of the harmony of religions. He believed that absolute truth is like an ocean and that any religion is a beach from which one can reach the sea, swim, or draw water. The essence and truth of all religions are the same. According to Ramakrishna, only ignorant people have religious prejudices and think that their religion is superior. Ramakrishna believed in the authenticity of all religions (Bhajanananda, 2013).

Ramakrishna went in different ways and believed that God could be reached by any means. He began his religious career with idolatry and the Bhakti, then with Tantra, then with monotheism, and finally with Yoga and the unity of existence. In Bhakti, there are two ways of worshiping Shiva and Vishnu. He went both ways. In Vaishnavism, there are two paths: a way to love Krishna and a way to love Ram. Ramakrishna went both ways. The two austerities of Tantra and Yoga are also different, but Ramakrishna used both austerities in the journey stages. Outside of Hinduism, he was devoted to the Buddha, *Mahavira*[7], *Guru Nanak*[8], and other *Sikh gurus*[9] (leaders). He considered the Sikh groups to be the embodiment of *Raja Janak*[10]. As already mentioned, Ramakrishna respected the religion of Islam and converted to Islam openly for a while. He also became interested in Christianity in 1874, and he considered Jesus a great yogi (Muller, 1899).

Unity of existence: Before explaining this topic, the researcher should state that the term unity of existence is related to Islamic philosophy and mysticism, which is also called the Unity of Being and Sufi metaphysics. The theory claims that the only actual existence in the universe belongs to God, and others are all manifestations and shadows of God. As a result, there is multiplicity in the universe, but this multiplicity is in manifestations. Existence is personal, but the multiplicity and variety of its types and effects are also preserved. One of the criticisms of Hinduism was the issue of polytheism. However, Ramakrishna and later his disciple Vivekananda reinterpreted this issue, an interpretation that they both offered is almost like the interpretation of Islam.

Ramakrishna shows that differences in religious attitudes are unrealistic, and differences are in interpretations and statements. He did not even see a difference between the theory of polytheism, monotheism, and the unity of existence. Ramakrishna believed that when we see ultimate reality in the dimension of the essence, we call it *Ashur, Paramatman, Allah*, or God. When we consider him in the dimension of attributes, we call him Creator, Almighty, Merciful and Compassionate or *Brahma, Shiva, Vishnu, Kali*; When we see him in the transcendental dimension of essence and discernment, we call him Brahman or (Gupta, 1983), according to Illuminations' philosophy, the light of lights. All three views are complementary, not contradictory.

Different levels of mind perceive God in different ways. God-worship at the level of the attitude of ordinary people is polytheism. At the grassroots level, people want tangible beliefs. This human sensibility has led to idolatry and polytheism (Maharaj, 2018).

Thinkers reach the level of unity and cognition of the essence of God and know God as the only essence. Mystics reach the transcendental level and perceive God as pure truth and ultimate reality. Ramakrishna considered the unity of existence in Vedanta to be the highest stage of cognition of God, but he believed that all three groups worshiped the same truth. If their worship is pure, salvation can be achieved from all three ways of polytheism, monotheism, and unity of existence (Maharaj, 2018).

Social Attitude of Ramakrishna

Unlike Ram Mohan Roy and Keshab Chandra Sen, Ramakrishna was a mystic and not a social reformer. He did not personally create any social reform movement. Of course, the movement named after him, created by his disciple Swami Vivekananda, did a valuable service to social reform that will be mentioned. After all, everyone has specific social positions and tendencies, and Ramakrishna is no exception (Rolland, 1929).

As a young man, he seems to have been loyal to India's particular class social system, the caste system. As mentioned earlier, Rani Rashmoni, who built Dakshineswar, Kali Temple, was Shudra. For this reason, no Brahman was willing to serve as a cleric in her temple. Ramakrishna's older brother accepted the position of a priest of the temple due to poverty. Ramakrishna was by no means ready to be in the temple with his brother; because he considered the food obtained there to be forbidden to him as a Brahman. Biographers and followers of Ramakrishna, such as Isherwood and *Swami Nikhilananda*, have admitted that Ramakrishna was arguing with his brother about this. Ramakrishna's stubborn support for the unjust caste system was one of his weaknesses (Isherwood, 1965).

In the following period, Ramakrishna lost his caste prejudices. During austerity, one day, his disciples saw him sweeping the house of one of the *Bhangies*[11]. He was very kind to the deprived. In 1861, Rani Rashmoni died and his son-in-law, *Mathuramohan*, became Lord of the region. He was a devotee of Ramakrishna. In 1868, he set out with Mathuramohan to visit the holy city of Varanasi. When passing through the villages of Bihar state, Ramakrishna first became acquainted with the extreme poverty of northern India. The area was suffering from famine at that time. Ramakrishna insisted on giving food to the poor. When Mathuramohan objected, Ramakrishna became very angry and said, you are a trustee of God! You must deliver that trust to the servants of God (Muller, 1899).

As Swami Nikhilananda points out, Ramakrishna's interest in the poor did not stem from socialist and scholastic attitudes such as socialism but his mystical attitude. According to the unity of existence, human beings are not servants of God but the manifestation of God. Ramakrishna saw a picture of Kali and Krishna in the poor and did not rest until he helped them (Nikhilananda, 1943).

Raising students and starting a movement

As a result of his acquaintance with the Brahmo Samaj organization, and especially Keshab Chandra Sen, Ramakrishna sought to establish a movement and nurture elite students, who later became the source of a widespread movement. His followers say that during the great ecstasy, he was also announced that great men who would change Indian society would join him as disciples. From 1875 onwards, Ramakrishna planned to train his disciples (Isherwood, 1965).

Ramakrishna gradually became known through the lectures of Keshab Chandra Sen in the Brahmo Samaj organization, and people went to the Kali Temple to see him.

The arrival of young people in Dakshineswar began in 1879. At that time, Ramakrishna had completed the stages of mystical conduct. The young people who became his disciples were educated and young, primarily aristocrats, intellectuals, or clerics. From 1879, disciples who had been preached to him in great ecstasy also came, each of whom later became a pillar of the Ramakrishna movement, led first by Narayan (Vivekananda), then by Kahl (Brahmananda) and Turk (Shivananda). Rama Krishna trained disciples who would later transform society (Rolland, 1929). The students arrived as follows:

1879:

Dr. Rajinder Dutt

Latu, Swami Adbhutananda, an employee of Ramchandran

Surendra Nath Mitra, a wealthy merchant

1881:

Rakhal Chandra Ghosh, Swami Brahmananda, the second leader of Ramakrishna Mission), is one of the great landlords.

Buro Gopal, Advaitananda, is one of the merchants.

Narendra Nath Datta, Swami Vivekananda, the great Indian thinker, became the first leader of Ramakrishna and succeeded Ramakrishna. He was an intellectual and belonged to the Kshatriya caste.

1882:

Mahendranath Gupta, author of the Gospel of Rama Krishna, known as "M." He was the headmaster of one of the schools.

Tarak Nath Ghosal, Swami Shivananda, who became the third leader of Rama Krishna Mishn after the death of Brahmananda, was a member of Brahmo Samaj and the son of a lawyer.

Yogindra Nath Choudhury, Swami Yogananda, was one of the aristocratic Brahmins.

Shashi Bhushan Chakravarty, Ramakrishnananda, was a faithful disciple and mystic.

Sarat Chandra Chakraborty, Saradananda, was the organization's first secretary for 25 years, and he has written the second person after Brahmananda and many works.

Kaliprasad Chandra, Swami Abhedananda, was the son of a Persian language teacher.

Harinath Chattopadhyay, Swami Turiyananda, was one of the famous mystics.

Gangadhar Ghatak, Swami Akhandananda, was a fourteen-year-old student.

Girish Chandra Ghosh was a seventeen-year-old student.

Balaram Bose was a wealthy man who spent his fortune founding the organization.

Nitya Niranjan Ghosh, Niranjanananda, was a young mystic.

Baburam Maharaj, Swami Premananda, was a 20-year-old student.

Tulasi Charan Dutta, Nirmalananda, is considered by some to be a disciple of Swami Vivekananda.

Durga Charan Nag was a senior householder student (Gambhirananda, 2018).

People who join Ramakrishna fall into three categories:

Public: Since 1880, when Ramakrishna became famous and mainly spoke about the miracles of Ramakrishna, hundreds of people came to visit him every day. Ramakrishna spends about twenty hours a day with the people and guides them with his simple mystical words (collected in the Ramakrishna Gospel Collection). His unique style was simplification and using proverbs and anecdotes (similar to Saadi style in Golestan) (Nikhilananda, 1943).

Householder disciples: After Keshab Chandra Sen promoted Ramakrishna's ideas, many intellectuals and families turned to him, and some of them became his permanent disciples. Of course, some of them, being homemakers and married, could not become *Sannyasi*[12]. One of the conditions of Sannyasa[13] and becoming a yogi is to leave all interests, spouse, children, and parents. Naturally, not everyone can do this. Among his extraordinary disciples were *Ram Chandra Datta and Manmohan Mittra* (Gupta, 1983).

Monk students: This group becomes the main disciples and flag bearers of the Ramakrishna movement. The names of those who have "*Nanda*" at the end (such as Vikikananda, Brahmananda, etc.) are from monks' disciples. When the seeker swears by giving up interests, he abandons the previous name and takes on a new name, as if he had been born again. The disciples of Ramakrishna and many other monks added the suffix Anand (meaning spiritual happiness). Anand is one of the good names of God in Indian mystical culture (Beckerlegge, 2000).

The number of such disciples of the monk was fifteen to twenty. However, these twenty people attracted millions of Indians and Westerners to Ramakrishna and founded the Ramakrishna Mission movement. A senior disciple of Ramakrishna, Swami Vivekananda, was the founder of the Ramakrishna Mission.

Before dying, Ramakrishna summoned Vivekananda, looked at him for a moment, and then went into ecstasy. When he comes out of ecstasy, the student's vision is also in ecstasy. "I transferred everything I had to my son; now I am nothing but a poor man, "maybe my son will do great things with the transferred force," he said. Finally, on August 15, 1886, this great mystic of contemporary India passed away (Isherwood, 1965).

Swami Vivekananda, the Great Modernist of Hinduism

Vivekananda, his original name Narendra Nath Datta (1863-1902, Calcutta), was a Hindu spiritual leader and reformer in India who sought to combine Indian spirituality with material progress of the West, claimed that the two complemented and supplemented each other.

Some consider Swami Vivekananda the highest Hindu thinker of the second millennium (after *Shankara and Ramanuja*[14]) and is arguably the most remarkable new theorist of Hinduism; His importance in contemporary Hinduism is similar to that of *Saint Paul* in Christianity (Rolland, 1997).

He was born into an upper-middle-class family of the *Kshatriya* caste in Bengal. There was an interest in the clergy and mysticism in the Vivekananda family. His father, *Vishwanath*, was influenced by the Brahmo Samaj reform movement. As mentioned in Vivekananda's biography, he was also in contact with Muslim mystics and intellectuals. The influence of Islamic thought and then acquaintance with Western thought caused him to find a reformist view of his religion. He opposed Sati and criticized idolatry. For the rest of his life, he was influenced by Islamic culture and even wore traditional Indian Islamic clothing (Nikhilananda, 1953).

Vivekananda attended a Western-style university focusing on Western philosophy, Christianity, and science. Gradually, social reforms became his most important concern. In addition, family teachings have not been ineffective in shaping his thoughts. He joined the Brahmo Samaj movement, which dealt with the abolition of child marriage, women's illiteracy, and the problems of the lower castes of society. He later became the most prominent disciple of Ramakrishna, who demonstrated the fundamental unity of all religions (Prabhananda, 2003).

He later became the foremost notable disciple of Ramakrishna, who proved the essential unity of all religions. The author will explain the influential philosophical concepts in religious and social life that Vivekananda has reinterpreted.

Reasons to prove the existence of God

Vivekananda does not personally seek to prove God because he believes that those who have come to understand God do not need proof, just like other holy books of other monotheistic religions that do not prove God. However, Vivekananda offers arguments for those who have not yet understood monotheism.

Causality: Vivekananda, in the book Jnana Yoga states that one of the reasons for the existence of God is the law of causality. He says that everything needs a cause to come into being. Also, logically, this series of causes must end in a cause, which is the absolute cause of God. This theory is similar to Farabi's theory of causality in Islamic philosophy.

Teleological argument: Vivekananda's Another argument for proving God is the Teleological argument. Accordingly, if we consider the universe as a system in which all the components work well together, we see order between them. Rationally, maintaining this order requires a superior organizer, which is the absolute power of God. The teleological argument first appears in the works of the Muslim philosopher Ibn Rushd (11AD) (Vivekananda, 1902).

The universe, in his view

From the worldview point of view, Vivekananda's view is a combination of a monotheistic view and existential unity. In the monotheistic view, the universe is God's creation, but in the view of the unity of existence, the universe is the manifestation of God. Nevertheless, in general, he is a neo-Vedanta and interprets the universe in the category of Shankara's unity of existence. Shankara said that there was no creation and that what we think of as creation is Maya or pure deception. Vivekananda adopts Shankara's idealistic view, but he mixes idealism with realism; He does not consider the world completely non-existent. The world is a manifestation of Brahman, which Maya has made an independent reality; However, it has no existential originality. This view seems contradictory, but Vivekananda solves this contradiction with an allegory.

The reality of the sea waves is nothing but the sea; they Have no independent origin; It is Maya. The waves merge with the sea in the blink of an eye, but at the same time, the shape of the waves is relatively original, which is a visible fact. In the same way, the relationship between the sea and the foam of the sea illuminates the relationship between the universe and God. Foam is nothing but water and is the natural result of the rising water. The universe is also the natural result of the roar of the ocean of absolute existence. However, foam is relatively original, visible, and has its own rules. Shankara considered the universe to be deceptive or Maya in general. Vivekananda believes this is not Vedanta's actual view. Ancient thinkers translated Mithya as deception. Mithya does not mean deception but finite, possible, non-absolute, and transient existence. The universe is not called Mithya because it is pure deception, but in the sense that its existence is finite and transient, it is called Mithya (Lal, 1976).

Swami Vivekananda reinterprets Maya. According to his theory, Maya is a reference to the principle of dialectics and contradiction in the universe, being or not being, ugliness or beauty, good or bad, everything is relative. Maya shows the contradictory nature of the universe.

We feel that the universe is original. While God, who is the original truth and reality, is incomprehensible and intuitive, what can be understood and observed is the universe. Vivekananda has said that the Maya interpretation is not that the universe is not authentic or is absolute non-existence. The universe is naturally genuine and original; For him, sometimes beyond the universe is deception. Maya expresses this contradiction. When we see the universe with the help of the five senses, it has a genuine existence; Because our five senses are a tool for understanding material and relative facts. If we had the sixth and seventh senses, we would see other facts, and we would probably realize the deception of the universe and the originality of Brahman. The universe is Maya because it has relative validity and originality, and everything is finite, mortal, and possible. We live in this mortal, finite and relative world. We are born in Maya; We live in Maya; All our worldly activities are Maya; All our knowledge is Maya. Actual existence is only God. There is nothing but God; If so, it is relative. The reality and originality of the universe are until we realize the absolute truth (Lal, 1976).

Vivekananda believes that in ignorance, man sees the phenomena of the universe but does not see God; When he sees God, the phenomena disappear for him completely; everything is only God. Maya theory is not the philosophy of justifying and interpreting the reality of the universe but the expression of reality. Everything in the universe is finite, possible, mortal, and relative. Swami Vivekananda says that Maya is not a theory of the interpretation of existence but an expression of its facts. Maya shows that the basis of our existence is non-contradiction. Being and not being, good and bad, ugly and beautiful, are together (Lal, 1976).

In the book Jnana Yoga, Swami Vivekananda identifies Maya with time, place, and causality. He describes the cycle of change from unity to plurality and how multiple manifestations of God have appeared. If we imagine the absolute as a and the existence as c, a to c comes through b, which is time-place-causality; In absolute truth, time, place, and causality have no meaning, but just as the roar of the sea raises the foam, God's creation has created, like foam, time, place, and causality, leading to the creation of the universe. The above cycle can be described as follows:

Time, place, and causality are relative truths and have no absolute originality. In the dream, man feels it is decades past, While the night is not over; Even in waking time, time depends on the mental state is slow or fast. Place, like time, is relative. Time is the distance between two stories. If there is complete stillness, time will not make sense; Space is measured concerning two points; there is no place if there are no points. Causality is also a mental matter. At the same time, all three elements have empirical reality, and they lose their identity only in the metaphysical dimension. Vivekananda, in Jnana Yoga, considers Maya to be the three elements of time, place, and causality.

So, what is the universe? Vivekananda says that the world is a collection of feelings of empirical sensations and findings of natural knowledge; The originality of the world is no more (Vivekananda, 1902).

Ramakrishna Mission (RKM)

Ramakrishna Mission is a global, non-political, non-sectarian spiritual organization engaged in various forms of humanitarian, social service activities for more than a century (since May 1, 1897). The monks of this organization serve millions of people without considering any distinction of caste, religion, or race (Beckerlegge, 2000).

Motto: The organization's motto is *ATMANO MOKSHARTHAM JAGAD HITAYA CHA*, "For one's own salvation and for the welfare of the world." Swami Vivekananda formulated it (Ramakrishna Mission, n.d.).

Emblem: Vivekananda interpretation of the emblem of Ramakrishna Mission:

"The wavy waters in the picture are symbolic of Karma, the lotus of Bhakti, and the rising-sun of Jnana. The encircling serpent is indicative of Yoga and awakened Kundalini Shakti, while the swan in the picture stands for *Paramatman*. Therefore, the idea of the picture is that by the union of Karma, Jnana, Bhakti, and Yoga, the vision of the Paramatman is obtained (Ramakrishna Mission, n.d.)."

Ideologies: The ideology of Ramakrishna Mishna, which is essentially the lifestyle of Sri Ramakrishna as expressed by Vivekananda, has three main characteristics:

1. This ideology presents the ancient principles of Vedanta in a modern way.
2. It is universal. It means it applies to all people of the world.
3. The principles of this ideology can also be used to solve everyday problems (Beckerlegge, 2000).

The fundamental maxims of this ideology are given below:

1. God-realization is the ultimate goal of life: One of the most important discoveries of ancient India is that the thinkers of that period realized that the whole universe is derived from an eternal and absolute power called Brahman. This pure power has both personal and impersonal aspects. The personal aspect is Ishwar, Kali, Allah, Shiva, Jehovah, and other names (Rolland, 1929)
2. Potential divinity of the soul: Brahman exists as the Atman in all people, the reason for the feeling of happiness and inner peace is also Brahman, but people turn to worldly pleasures due to neglect and ignorance of it, and it can be said that ignorance is the source of all suffering. The less ignorance there is, the more the Atman manifests himself, and this is a manifestation of the potential divinity of the soul that is the essence of true religion (Ramakrishna Mission, n.d.).

3. Synthesis of the Yoga: According to Ramakrishna and Vivekananda, it is possible to eliminate ignorance and manifestation of the inner divinity that leads to God-realization through Yoga. As mentioned earlier, we have four main types of Yoga. Each of them is an independent means of understanding God. Nevertheless, because each one alone is for developing a particular part of the soul and mind, people must act in all four ways to achieve balance and Atman (Ramakrishna Mission, n.d.).
4. Morality based on Strength: According to Vivekananda, the leading cause of suffering, pain, and immorality in life is weakness, and the main reason for weakness is ignorance of Atman. Awareness of Atman gives man the strength to overcome fear and weakness and helps man to have a better life. Vivekananda believed that all people have much potential, but they cannot actualize it because of fear and weakness. If people know Atman, they can easily show their potential. Vivekananda calls this process Man-Making Education (Ramakrishna Mission, n.d.).
5. Harmony of Religions: It is stated in the Vedas that Reality is known by different names. It is also said in the Gita that different spiritual paths lead to the same destination. Using these two propositions, Ramakrishna proved that all religions pursue the same goal and that all religions in the world are equal. This issue is divided into harmony within Hinduism and harmony among world religions (Maharaj, 2018).

Harmony within Hinduism: Ramakrishna did not follow a particular sect of Hinduism but accepted it all. He believed that all sects of Hinduism, such as Dualism, Non-dualism, and others, represent different Reality stages.

Harmony among world religions: Ramakrishna respected the differences of all religions but believed that the goal of all religions is to reach the ultimate truth, Brahma. Ramakrishna had a famous principle: Yato mat, Tato path (As many faiths, so many paths). In addition, Vivekananda believed that all the world's religions represented a universal and eternal religion. He considered Vedanta to be that religion and believed that Vedanta could be the basis of all religions (Maharaj, 2018).

A New Definition of Work: Swami Vivekananda has defined work in a new way, which is the role model of Ramakrishna Mission.

All work is sacred: According to Nivedita[15], there is no distinction between the sacred and the secular. It means that all work is sacred, even daily and simple works like sweeping (Ramakrishna Mission, 2021).

Work is a kind of worship: The Gita talks about work in chapter 18, verse 46: “By performing one’s natural occupation, one worships the creator from whom all living entities have come into being, and by whom the whole universe is pervaded. By such performance of work, a person quickly attains perfection.” Based on this statement, Vivekananda considers working a kind of worship (Fosse, 2007).

Serving Man is service to God: As mentioned earlier, Ramakrishna believed that people are the manifestation of God and his disciple, Vivekananda, followed his way. There is a quote from Ramakrishna: ‘Shiva Jnane Jiva Seva.’ It means service to Man is service to Shiva (Hindu God) (Vivekananda, 2019).

The main focus of work should be on poor people: “He who sees Shiva in the poor, in the weak and the diseased, really worships Shiva; and Shiva is more pleased with him than with the man who sees Him only in temples.” Vivekananda said. It can be said that Swami Vivekananda was the first religious reformer and leader that paid attention to poor people (Vivekananda, 2019).

Work is a spiritual discipline: When we consider doing work as worship of God, we try to do it in the best way, then it becomes a spiritual discipline or Yoga. In other words, the mind becomes purified, and the potential divinity of the soul manifests itself more and more. So, works that are done as worship benefit the doer too. Also, understanding work as a spiritual discipline is called Karma Yoga (Ramakrishna Mission, 2021).

Features and Activities: Ramakrishna Mission shows its ideology through different activities; these activities vary from health to education, women issues, self-employment, progress in villages, manner, spiritual guidance, and helping victims. These activities are considered as services to God through humans. Ramakrishna believes that servicing is not limited to some activities and timing, but it is the lifestyle. Like Monks that may not do services in society, they do within the monastic society without any limitation or time pressure until they are physically able to do these. Giving service in Ramakrishna Mission has its characteristics that will be mentioned below:

1. Love, devotion, generosity: Devotion is an essential part of the *Holy Trio*[16], and it is the first step in the spiritual paths of Bhakti, Karma, and Jnana. Monks of Mission consider their Sangha[17] as the mythical body of Sri Ramakrishna, they are trained to compound their sensuality in

the collective will of Sangha, and their activities and results are granted to God as their worship. Members of Ramakrishna Mission do not get credit for what they do; the credits are for Sangha. What they do, is not for their glory; monks of Ramakrishna order practice self-analysis and work on knowing themselves with the inner self that never changes. Monks practice unselfishness. As mentioned earlier, one of Ramakrishna principles is to serve God, although it is hard to serve all sick or poor people, for this aim needs lots of sacrifice such as time, ease, energy, etc. in such activities, they do not expect to be famous, or any rewards from others and only work for God and as they said, love is their motivation (Ramakrishna Mission, 2021).

2. Liberty, Fraternity, and Equality: human has wished these three elements during history; the Ramakrishna Mission claims that they could make it a reality in its society, as Swami Vivekananda mentions that "liberty is the first condition of growth." Society needs to be relieved from religious bigotry and hatred. In other words, freedom of belief and thoughts is an aim of the Ramakrishna movement. Ramakrishna Mission wants comfort for people; equally, no caste, no difference between people no matter if they are Brahmin or Dalit, poor or rich, they all are considered Divin's children. To make equality in society, those at lower levels should be raised to balance (Ramakrishna Mission, 2021).
3. Excellence, Teamwork, Efficiency: Ramakrishna Mission governs its activities with these principles. The members believe that they must do their activities as better as possible because they give these to God. Moreover, teamwork is a vital component for members of the mission (Ramakrishna Mission, 2021).
4. Transparency, Honesty, Truthfulness: One of the most vital principles of this mission is transparency in financial affairs. Therefore, all financial functions, such as depositing donations and allocating funds to different goals of the mission, are presented to the audience in detail (Ramakrishna Mission, 2021).
5. Social commitment without politics: Ramakrishna Mission tries to keep its position aside from policies because it is a spiritual organization (Ramakrishna Mission, 2021).

The activities by Ramakrishna Mission can be categorized as follow:

1. Relief and Rehabilitation work: since 1897, this organization has been bestowed on victims of natural disasters and riots (Ramakrishna Mission, 2019).
2. Medical services: Ramakrishna Mission has 100 dispensaries, 14 hospitals, and over 50 mobile dispensaries. These places are primarily for poor people located in different places. Many patients have already used these centers for treatments, and even operations have been done freely. About 700 students are training annually for these centers (Ramakrishna Mission, 2014).
3. Educational works: According to the annual report of the Ramakrishna Mission, it has established one university with seven colleges, they had established over 500 schools, two language schools, 100 hostels even centers for the disabled (Ramakrishna Mission, 2006).
4. Work in rural and tribal areas: Ramakrishna Mission has established two agriculture institutions for rural and tribal people; also, they introduce farmers to the latest methods of agriculture and new technologies; they support farmers financially to improve their job. There are other projects such as building houses and toilets, soil testing, wasteland developments, planting, providing drinking water, and other projects like those that have been mentioned (Ramakrishna Mission, 2019).
5. Welfare work: the Ramakrishna Mission gives financial aid to students and low-income families, additionally providing medical services for them (Ramakrishna Mission, 2018).
6. Work for women: this organization has done many activities for women, from those who want to give birth to elderlies by providing retirement homes, establishing training centers for women, and paying widows (Ramakrishna Mission, 2017).
7. Activities for youngsters: the Ramakrishna Mission pays attention to the spiritual training of youths, not only mythical and spiritual but also provides places for entertainment and cultural training. The youngsters' activities in these centers are singing, gaming, telling stories, and sessions about ethical life, culture, and so on (Ramakrishna Mission, 2013).
8. Spreading religion and culture: for reaching this aim, Ramakrishna Mission has established many libraries, museums, exhibitions and also has held seminars and speeches for audiences. They even publish magazines and books about Vedanta, Holy mother[18] , and other such cases in different languages (Ramakrishna Mission, 2020)

9. Spiritual services: they have places to do their worships; for example, they sing some chants every evening, they also have different plans for the holidays such as Ramakrishna's birthday, and thousands of people join these mythical programs. They hold speaking sessions about different spiritual subjects, also the most important spiritual activities are held by the president, vice president, and senior monks of Ramakrishna Mission (Ramakrishna Mission, 2019)
10. Activities out of India: Vedanta philosophy was spread to the West by Swami Vivekananda for the first time in New York. Today this kind of training has been improved and turned to a flowing thought as 'Vedanta movement, and there are 13 Vedanta associations in New York now. Most activities are mythical, but other services are in Bangladesh, South Africa, and Sri Lanka. It should be mentioned that the Ramakrishna Mission does not do any advertising activities (Ramakrishna Mission, 2006).

Similarities between Islamic attitudes and attitudes of the Ramakrishna Mission

One of the questions of this research is to investigate the relationship between the teachings of Islam and the Ramakrishna Mission. To answer this question, the researcher will first outline the possible contexts of this relationship and then introduce the similarities between the two.

Islam entered the Indian subcontinent in the 7th century when the Arabs conquered Sindh, and later reached northern India through the *Ghorian* conquest in the 12th century, and has since become part of India's religious and cultural heritage (Anjum, 2012).

From the 12th century onwards, it can be considered the beginning of Muslim rule in the subcontinent, which was often in the north or south of the subcontinent, such as the Sultanate of Deccan, the Sultanate of Mysore, the Sultanate of Bahmani, the Mughal Empire, the Sultanate of Bengal and the Sultanate of Gujarat. Some Muslim rulers had religious prejudices, such as Aladdin Khaliji, but others, such as Akbar, chose secular rule.

Muslim rule in India led to extending of Islam to the people so that native Muslim monarchies were formed. Such as Deccan, Bengal, Gujarat (Syed et al., 2011).

After the Vedic period, the caste system gradually changed, and living conditions became tough for the lower castes and Dalits. Therefore, they converted to other religions such as Jainism, Islam, and Buddhism to escape the harsh conditions of the caste system. It may be concluded that those who converted to other religions such as Islam and became acquainted with these religions were better able to understand the discrimination in the Hindu system.

One of the most important reasons for the influence of Islam on Hindu reform movements can be traced to the number of Muslims in India and the geographical dispersion of Islam in the subcontinent. Nor can it be said that the high Muslim population of India is only due to Muslim governments, but when we examine the geographical dispersion of the Muslim population of India, we will see Despite the absence of an Islamic government in some regions, the Muslim population is significant (Gokhale, 1965).

Moreover, after examining the Hindu reform movements that took shape in the fourteenth to sixteenth centuries, we find that their leaders were directly inspired by Islam and Muslim mystics. For example, one of the great religious leaders whose works show the undeniable influence of Islam is Guru Nanak (1469-1539). The Sikh religion, founded by Nanak, is distinguished by its militant faction against Islam but is essentially a product of the historical circumstances of the 17th century. Nanak's goal was to unite both Hindus and Islam by appealing to what they both know to be fundamental truths. He considers Kabir (One of the great Muslim mystics) his spiritual teacher, and their teachings are very similar. His debt to Islam is expressed in his emphasis on the will and greatness of God, while the basic structure of thought, with its desire for total unity, reflects his Hindu heritage (Gokhale, 1965).

Also, as mentioned earlier, Ramakrishna converted to Islam for a time; he did thorough research on Islam and Islamic mysticism, followed the rules of Islam, and even ate beef. In mysticism, he was also able to reach high levels of Islamic mysticism. In other words, he was thoroughly acquainted with Islam.

Familiarity with Islam also applies to Vivekananda because he and his family were in contact with Muslim thinkers and leaders.

Apart from the historical background of Islam's influence on Hindu reforms, when we examine the basic principles of the Ramakrishna Mission, we notice the similarities between the teachings of Islam and the principles of the Ramakrishna Mission. In this section, we will examine the similarities between the teachings of Islam and the principles of Ramakrishna. (Note: The author has directly used the verses of the Qur'an as the most reliable Muslim source for comparison).

Liberty, Fraternity, and Equality: Above, when we examined Ramakrishna's social attitude, we stated that he was opposed to the caste system (after reaching mystical authorities), but not from a political or sociological point of view, but he believed that we are all representatives of God and His manifestation on earth. He also treated all people equally, including the Dalits. On the other hand, the Holy Qur'an emphasizes the equality of human beings in various verses such as "O people, we created you from the same male and a female and rendered you distinct peoples and tribes that you may recognize one another. The best among you in the sight of God is the most righteous. God is Omniscient, Cognizant (Quran 49: 13, Universal Unity edition)[19]." According to the commentators, this verse has emphasized its condemnation of arrogance and class, racial and relative superiority (Tabatabaei, 1971). The Quran also emphasizes respect for all people: we have honored the children of Adam and provided them with rides on land and in the sea. We provided for them good provisions, and we gave them greater advantages than many of our creatures (Quran 17: 70, Universal Unity edition)[20]. According to the commentators, the meaning of these verses is appropriate for the equality of all human beings in enjoying the essential individual and collective rights, such as the right to life, financial and life security, the right to possess and acquire, the right to work and the right to wages and other fundamental rights and freedoms. It is the view of Islam (Al Bagha, 1983).

Harmony of religions: Regarding this subject, Ramakrishna believed that all religions are equal and that the destination of all of them is the same. The Qur'an does not mention the equality of all religions, but all monotheistic religions are respected. The followers of these religions will prosper, "Indeed the faithful, the Jews, the Christians, and the Sabaeans—those of them who have faith in Allah and the Last Day and act righteously—they shall have their reward from their Lord, and they will have no fear, nor will they grieve (Quran 2:62, Universal Unity edition)[21]." Nevertheless, the second proposition, that the destination of all religions is the same, is also mentioned in the Qur'an (reaching the pure truth and reaching God). For example: "I did not create the jinn and the humans except that they may worship Me (Quran 51:56, Universal Unity edition)[22]."

God-realization is the ultimate goal of life: There are many verses in the Qur'an regarding knowing and attaining God; The ultimate goal of life in Islam can be found by examining the following verses. "I did not create the jinn and the humans except that they may worship Me (Quran 51:56, Universal Unity edition)", "And that you worship [only] Me? This is a straight path (Quran 36: 61, Universal Unity edition)[23]", "And that to your Lord ˹alone˺ is the ultimate return ˹of all things˺ (Quran 53:42, Universal Unity edition)[24]", "Are they waiting for Allah ˹Himself˺ to come to them in the shade of clouds, along with the angels? ˹If He did˺, then the matter would be settled ˹at once˺. And to Allah ˹all˺ matters will be returned ˹for judgment˺ (Quran 2:210, Universal Unity edition)[25], "To Allah ˹alone˺ belongs the knowledge of what is hidden in the heavens and the earth. And to Him all matters are returned. So, worship Him and put your trust in Him. And your Lord is never unaware of what you do (Quran 11:123, Universal Unity edition)[26]". As it is clear from the mentioned verses, the ultimate goal of man and life is to reach God and know him. In addition, in most verses of the Qur'an, God invites man to think about the signs of existence and that there is a single Creator who created all beings.

Concept of work: About 400 verses of the Qur'an express the importance and value of work (Nadali, 2012). For example: "Indeed, your efforts are diverse (Quran 92:4 Universal Unity edition)[27]", "But whoever desires the Hereafter and strives for it accordingly, and is a ˹true˺ believer, it is they whose striving will be appreciated (Quran 17:19 Universal Unity edition)[28]", "And that there is not for man except that [good] for which he strives. And that his effort is going to be seen. Then they will be fully rewarded (Quran 53:39-41 Universal Unity edition)[29]", "Every soul will be detained for what it has done (Quran 74: 38 Universal Unity edition)[30]". The Prophet Muhammad and the Imams also emphasized the value of work as worship. For instance, according to Prophet Muhammad, worship is seventy parts, the best of which is the lawful acquisition (al-Kulayni, 2012). Additionally, Imam Ali narrated from the prophet Mohamad that "One who meets the needs of his religious brother is like one who has worshiped God all his life (Majlesi, 1996)." Regarding the importance of work, Imam Ali says that "one who seeks a lawful day is like a mujahid in the way of God (Maghrebi, 2005)."

Excellence, Teamwork, Efficiency: Teamwork and consulting with each other is another issue that is also mentioned in the Qur'an. The Qur'an also mentions the need for teamwork for the salvation of society; for more clarification, note the following verses. "And cooperate in righteousness and piety, but do not cooperate in sin and aggression. And fear Allah; indeed, Allah is severe in penalty (Quran 5:2, Universal Unity edition)[31]", "And hold firmly to the rope of Allah1 and do not be divided. Remember Allah's favor upon you when you were enemies, then He united your hearts, so you—by His grace—became brothers. And you were at the brink of a fiery pit, and He saved you from it. This is how Allah makes His revelations clear to you, so that you may be ˹rightly˺ guided (Quran 3:103, Universal Unity edition)[32]", "Let there be a group among you who call ˹others˺ to goodness, encourage what is good, and forbid what is evil—it is they who will be successful (Quran 3:104, Universal Unity edition)[33]", "who respond to their Lord, establish prayer, conduct their affairs by mutual consultation, and donate from what We have provided for them (Quran 42:38, Universal Unity edition)[34]".

From the above studies and the chronological precedence of Islam over the reform movements of Hinduism, it can be concluded that the teachings of Islam and the Qur'an have been influential in the growth of the Ramakrishna organization.

Conclusion of Chapter

At the end of this chapter, it is better to mention a few critical points:

The creativity of the Ramakrishna movement was in reinterpreting Hindu sacred scriptures, Vedas and Bhagavad Gita. In this regard, the influence of Islam on the leaders of Ramakrishna Mission, Ramakrishna, and Vivekananda, cannot be denied, as mentioned in the text.

Some theories of the Ramakrishna movement have been based on the Islamic monotheistic view, for example, the theory of the Compatibility of monotheism and the unity of existence, or as another example, we can mention work ideology.

Inspired by the teachings of other religions, they were able to offer a new definition of the Gita and the Vedas. It can be said that the teachings of other religions forced them to refer to the original texts of Hinduism and get rid of superstitions and misinterpretations.

[1] According to Hindu Caste System, Shudra, Dalits (Untouchables) are out of Caste and they are impure. Also, whatever they touch is impure too.

[2] pure existence

[3] pure consciousness

[4] pure happiness

[5] Indian mystics

[6] The second stage of Samadhi is called Nirvikalpa Samadhi or great ecstasy.

[7] Mahavira was the 24th Tirthankara (a saviour and spiritual teacher) of Jainism.

[8] Guru Nanak was the founder of Sikhism and is the first of the ten Sikh Gurus.

[9] Guru means a Hindu spiritual teacher.

[10] Raja Janak or Janaka was king of Mithila (Videha) and the father of Sita (wife of Ram), the key character of the Hindu epic Ramayana.

[11] Valmiki, also known as Bhanghi and Balmiki, is a Dalit caste (Untouchable) in India and Pakistan.

[12] A person who practices Sannyasa.

[13] Sannyasa is a form of asceticism, is marked by the renunciation of material desires and prejudices, represented by a state of disinterest and detachment from material life, and has the purpose of spending one's life in peaceful, spiritual pursuits.

[14] Indian philosophers

[15] Nivedita was an Irish teacher, author, social activist, school founder and disciple of Swami Vivekananda. Her real name was Margaret Elizabeth Noble, after meeting Swami Vivekananda, he gave her the name Nivedita (meaning Dedicated to God).

[16] Ramakrishna, Sarada Devi (wife of Ramakrishna) and Vivekananda are known as Holy Trio.

[17] Sangha is a Sanskrit word that means Association or Community.

[18] Holy Mother is wife of Ramakrishna, Sarada Devi.

[19] آیه 13 سوره مبارکه حجرات: يَا أَيُّهَا النَّاسُ إِنَّا خَلَقْنَاكُمْ مِنْ ذَكَرٍ وَأُنْثَىٰ وَجَعَلْنَاكُمْ شُعُوبًا وَقَبَائِلَ لِتَعَارَفُوا ۚ إِنَّ أَكْرَمَكُمْ عِنْدَ اللَّهِ أَتْقَاكُمْ ۚ إِنَّ اللَّهَ عَلِيمٌ خَبِيرٌ.

[20] آیه 70 سوره مبارکه أسراء: وَلَقَدْ كَرَّمْنَا بَنِي آدَمَ وَحَمَلْنَاهُمْ فِي الْبَرِّ وَالْبَحْرِ وَرَزَقْنَاهُمْ مِنَ الطَّيِّبَاتِ وَفَضَّلْنَاهُمْ عَلَىٰ كَثِيرٍ مِمَّنْ خَلَقْنَا تَفْضِيلًا.

[21] آیه 62 سوره مبارکه بقره: إِنَّ الَّذِينَ آمَنُوا وَالَّذِينَ هَادُوا وَالنَّصَارَىٰ وَالصَّابِئِينَ مَنْ آمَنَ بِاللَّهِ وَالْيَوْمِ الْآخِرِ وَعَمِلَ صَالِحًا فَلَهُمْ أَجْرُهُمْ عِنْدَ رَبِّهِمْ وَلَا خَوْفٌ عَلَيْهِمْ وَلَا هُمْ يَحْزَنُونَ

[22] آیه 56 سوره مبارکه ذاریات: وَمَا خَلَقْتُ الْجِنَّ وَالْإِنْسَ إِلَّا لِيَعْبُدُونِ

[23] آیه 61 سوره مبارکه یس: وَأَنِ اعْبُدُونِي ۚ هَٰذَا صِرَاطٌ مُسْتَقِيمٌ

[24] آیه 42 سوره مبارکه نجم: وَأَنَّ إِلَىٰ رَبِّكَ الْمُنْتَهَىٰ

[25] آیه 210 سوره مبارکه بقره: هَلْ يَنْظُرُونَ إِلَّا أَنْ يَأْتِيَهُمُ اللَّهُ فِي ظُلَلٍ مِنَ الْغَمَامِ وَالْمَلَائِكَةُ وَقُضِيَ الْأَمْرُ ۚ وَإِلَى اللَّهِ تُرْجَعُ الْأُمُورُ

[26] آیه 123 سوره مبارکه هود: وَلِلَّهِ غَيْبُ السَّمَاوَاتِ وَالْأَرْضِ وَإِلَيْهِ يُرْجَعُ الْأَمْرُ كُلُّهُ فَاعْبُدْهُ وَتَوَكَّلْ عَلَيْهِ ۚ وَمَا رَبُّكَ بِغَافِلٍ عَمَّا تَعْمَلُونَ

[27] آیه 4 سوره مبارکه لیل: إِنَّ سَعْيَكُمْ لَشَتَّىٰ

[28] آیه 19 سوره مبارک اسراء: وَمَنْ أَرَادَ الْآخِرَةَ وَسَعَىٰ لَهَا سَعْيَهَا وَهُوَ مُؤْمِنٌ فَأُولَٰئِكَ كَانَ سَعْيُهُمْ مَشْكُورًا

[29] آیات 39 تا 41 سوره مبارکه نجم: وَأَنْ لَيْسَ لِلْإِنْسَانِ إِلَّا مَا سَعَىٰ. وَأَنَّ سَعْيَهُ سَوْفَ يُرَىٰ. ثُمَّ يُجْزَاهُ الْجَزَاءَ الْأَوْفَىٰ

[30] آیه 38 سوره مبارکه مدثر: كُلُّ نَفْسٍ بِمَا كَسَبَتْ رَهِينَةٌ

[31] آیه 2 سوره مبارکه مائده: وَتَعَاوَنُوا عَلَى الْبِرِّ وَالتَّقْوَىٰ ۖ وَلَا تَعَاوَنُوا عَلَى الْإِثْمِ وَالْعُدْوَانِ ۚ وَاتَّقُوا اللَّهَ ۖ إِنَّ اللَّهَ شَدِيدُ الْعِقَابِ

[32] آیه 103 سوره مبارکه آلعمران: وَاعْتَصِمُوا بِحَبْلِ اللَّهِ جَمِيعًا وَلَا تَفَرَّقُوا ۚ وَاذْكُرُوا نِعْمَتَ اللَّهِ عَلَيْكُمْ إِذْ كُنْتُمْ أَعْدَاءً فَأَلَّفَ بَيْنَ قُلُوبِكُمْ فَأَصْبَحْتُمْ بِنِعْمَتِهِ إِخْوَانًا وَكُنْتُمْ عَلَىٰ شَفَا حُفْرَةٍ مِنَ النَّارِ فَأَنْقَذَكُمْ مِنْهَا ۗ كَذَٰلِكَ يُبَيِّنُ اللَّهُ لَكُمْ آيَاتِهِ لَعَلَّكُمْ تَهْتَدُونَ

[33] آیه 104 سوره مبارکه آلعمران: وَلْتَكُنْ مِنْكُمْ أُمَّةٌ يَدْعُونَ إِلَى الْخَيْرِ وَيَأْمُرُونَ بِالْمَعْرُوفِ وَيَنْهَوْنَ عَنِ الْمُنْكَرِ ۚ وَأُولَٰئِكَ هُمُ الْمُفْلِحُونَ

[34] آیه 38 سوره مبارکه شوری: وَالَّذِينَ اسْتَجَابُوا لِرَبِّهِمْ وَأَقَامُوا الصَّلَاةَ وَأَمْرُهُمْ شُورَىٰ بَيْنَهُمْ وَمِمَّا رَزَقْنَاهُمْ يُنْفِقُونَ

IV

Paramahamsa Yogananda (SRF)

In this chapter, the movement we will examine is the Paramahamsa Yogananda religious movement. The importance of this movement is due to its breadth (east to west) and its newness. Many people follow the teachings of Yogananda. In addition to the breadth and novelty of the Yogananda movement, it should be noted that the strength of the Yogananda movement is the combination of modern science and the ancient teachings of Hinduism, which is what makes Yogananda so successful famous in the west.

So, in this chapter we will first introduce the character of Paramahamsa Yogananda, his movement (Self-Realization Fellowship), his books and the teachings of Yogananda. Finally, we examine the similarities between Islamic teachings and Yogananda beliefs.

Introducing Paramahamsa Yogananda

Mukunda Lal Ghosh (Paramahamsa Yogananda) was born on January 5, 1893, in Gorakhpur, India, to a religious and prosperous Bengali family. His followers claim that it was apparent to those around him that his depth of knowledge and spiritual experience was far beyond the ordinary from his childhood.

Both of his parents were disciples of *Lahiri Mahasaya*[1], a famous master who was involved in the reintroduction of *Kriya Yoga* in modern India.

When Yogananda was a child, *Lahiri Mahasaya* blessed him and told her mother that he would be a yogi and lead many people to God (Yogananda, 2005).

As a young man, Yogananda traveled to many parts of India in the hope of finding a teacher to guide him in his spiritual path. In 1910, at the age of seventeen, he met and became a disciple of *Swami Sri Yukteswar Giri*[2], one of the most important masters of yoga. Yogananda received ten years of hard yoga training from this master. At the very first meeting with Mukunda and on other occasions, Sri Yukteswar Giri told him that he had been chosen to promote the science of yoga in the west (Yogananda, 2005).

Due to his spiritual character, Yogananda did not show much interest in school. However, as he had promised his father, he finished high school in 1910 and went to *Sri Bharat Dharam Maha Mandal* temple in Varanasi. Nevertheless, it was tough for him to stay away from his family (Yogananda, 2005).

Upon entering the temple, he had a good relationship with *Swami Dayananda*, the temple leader, but others mocked him because they thought he had to do all the temple works all the time. *Swami Dayananda* helped and guided her in meditating and concentrating (Yogananda, 2005).

Sometime later, when Yogananda was shopping, he saw a monk and felt he had to go to him. He was the same master who had seen his face thousands of times in his revelations, Swami Sri Yukteswar Giri, a monk from the temple of Sarampur. After four weeks, Yogananda went to Sarampur and saw his master. The master told him that he should go to Calcutta and study at the university because one day he will go to the west, and if he has a university degree as a Hindu, it will be easier for the people of the west to accept the ancient Hindu religion (Yogananda, 2005).

Yogananda graduated from Calcutta University in June 1915. Other professors and students did not think he could even pass the final exams.

Yogananda says about his master: I was always excited to sit next to Swami Sri Yukteswar Giri. The disciple gains spiritual strength from communicating with the master; Because a subtle current of electricity is produced in its existence. It is as if the mechanism of unpleasant habits is melted in the disciple's brain and fails, and his worldly tendencies disappear. At least for a moment, he may feel that the veil of Maya has been removed from his eyes and experience a moment of divine joy. Whenever I sat in front of my master in the traditional Indian way, my whole body was filled with liberating radiation (Yogananda, 2005).

Yogananda wanted permission from a master to meditate in the Himalayas, so he approached *Ram Gopal Mazumdar*, who lived in a village near the famous *Tarakeswar* Temple. He found the village with great difficulty, and on the way to that village, he met a man who was the same Ram Gopal or the saint who was always awake. On his way to the hut, Ram Gopal told Yogananda, you seem to be running away from your master; While he has all the features you need. You must return to him; the mountains cannot be your master. So, the second Yogananda master was Ram Gopal (Neumann, 2019).

After graduation, his father wanted him to take over the management of the Bengal-Nagpur Railway, but he flatly rejected the offer and instead went to the temple and asked the master to introduce him to the monastic system formally. The master accepted it. Thus, he entered the monastic system in July 1915. He describes this day as follows:

On the inner porch of Sarampur Monastery, the master dipped a new white silk shawl in ocher[3]. When the cloth was dry, the master wrapped it around my body as a garment to forget the world. Then he added: One day, you will go to the west. They prefer silk. Instead of the usual cotton fabric, I have chosen this silk fabric to symbolize you. The master allowed him to choose his new name as a monk, and he chose Yogananda, which means happiness and bliss through divine connection (Yogananda, 2005).

Yogananda belonged to the *Giri* branch of the monastic system. This system, which has a long history in India, is being reorganized by *Shankaracharya*. The sacred teachers of this branch are called *Jagat Guru Sri Shankaracharya*. All monks swear to abstain from attachment, chastity, and obedience to their spiritual master. Each Swami adds a word to his new name that indicates his official connection to one of the ten branches of the monastic system. *Giri, Sagar, Bharati, Puri, Saraswati, Aryana,* and *Tirtha* branches are inclouding(Neumann, 2019).

There is a difference between a Swami and a Yogi: A Swami is not necessarily a Yogi. A Yogi uses one of the scientific techniques to reach God. He can be single or married, have worldly responsibilities, or even be bound by one official ritual. Swami may take the path of simply forgetting the world, but Yogi takes a step-by-step approach that prepares his body and mind for his soul to be gradually liberated. Therefore, he does not accept anything just because of faith or emotions and interests without any reason (Neumann, 2016).

Yogananda went to the United States in 1920 and returned to India fifteen years later. At this time, he received the monastic title of *Paramahamsa* from his master Swami Sri Yukteswar Giri. *Para* means Superior, and *Hamsa* means swan. Mythologically, the swan is a symbol of *Brahma*. This title comes before his name and replaces the previous title, Swami. After giving him this title, his master said: My work in this world is over, and from now on, you must continue it. Please send someone to *Puri* to take charge of the *Ashram*. I leave everything to you. I am sure you can bring the boat of your life and the organization to a safe shore (Neumann, 2016).

His third teacher, who profoundly influenced Yogananda's spiritual thought, was *Lahiri Mahasaya*. One of the essential features of his life was inviting followers of different religions to *Kriya Yoga*. It did not matter whether his disciples were Hindu, Muslim, or Christian. However, he belonged to the caste of Brahmins or not. Lahiri Mahasaya boldly tried to dispel the caste prejudice that was so prevalent during his lifetime; In such a way that his teachings influenced everyone from every sect and race. He always said to his disciples: Remember that you do not belong to anyone, and no one belongs to you. Do not forget that you will suddenly leave everything in this world one day, so grow the love of God in yourself from now on. Be ready to accept death every day and be aware of it. Unfortunately, you think of yourself only as a body. Always meditate and imagine yourself as an infinite essence and free yourself from any inferiority, do not let yourself be trapped by the body, and let Kriya Yoga be your guide so that you can go to God (Yogananda, 2005).

So Yogananda has benefited from three masters. The first is Swami Sri Yukteswar Giri, and the second is Ram Gopal, and the third is Lahiri Mahasaya Yukteswar Giri greatly influenced the spirit of Yogananda, and Yogananda learned Kriya Yoga from him.

West World and Self-Realization Fellowship (SRF)

Yukteswar Giri once asked Yogananda: Why do you avoid organizational work? He replied: Master! This kind of work is not appreciated. Whatever the head of the organization does, he will be criticized. The master said: Do you want all the divine mysticism to be given only to you? If it were not for the teachers who teach their knowledge to others, could you or anyone else reach God through yoga? Master's deep counsel shook him, so he tried as much as he could to teach his fellow man the liberating truths he had learned from his masters (Yogananda, 2005). Yogananda's first work is as follows:

The ideal of proper education for young children had always attracted his attention. He saw the futile results of teachings that focused only on the growth of the body. The place of moral and spiritual values without which no human being can taste happiness was empty among the formal lessons. He decided to establish a school where young boys could become real human beings. The first step in this direction began with seven students in a village in Bengal. It is worth mentioning that the number of his students was increasing every day (Neumann, 2019).

The following year (1918), through the generosity of *Maharaja Sir Manindra Chandra Nandy, Maharaja of Cossimbazar Raj*, he was able to move the group of boys to *Ranchi[4]*. The Cossimbazar Palace in Ranchi also became the main school building. Yogananda had a curriculum for elementary and high school, including agriculture, industry, commerce, and general education. In presenting all these lessons, the ancient method of the monk system was also included. He held most of his classes outdoors. In addition, students were taught meditation, yoga, and a particular health system, which is the principle of yoga that Yogananda discovered in 1918 (Neumann, 2019).

Initially, Ranchi School, which was simple and small, became an institution and became famous in Bihar and Bengal. Many sections of the school were run with the financial support of volunteers who respected the continuing educational aspirations of the ancient masters. Two new branches of this school were established in *Midnapore and Lakshmanpur*. This school is one of the branches of the association known today as *the Yogada Satsanga Society of India*, founded in 1917 by Yogananda. Society has another branch in Ranchi, Bihar. In addition to meditation centers, the association has 21 educational institutions, ranging from elementary to pre-university. The word *Satsanga* means companionship with God. Paramahamsa Yogananda translated the Hindi word for Westerners as Self-Realization Fellowship (Pokazanyeva, 2015).

Yogananda's next move was to go to the United States. He was invited to speak at the International Congress of Spirituality in Boston. He came to America alone, and he did not know anyone there. However, he found thousands there, ready and eager for the eternal teachings of Kriya Yoga. He left India in August 1920 and sailed for the United States. During the two-month voyage, he spoke to the ship's passengers in English, which earned him several invitations to speak to various groups in the United States (Pokazanyeva, 2015).

He spoke at the Boston Spiritual Congress on October 6, 1920. This speech was welcomed. He then lived in Boston for three years. He gave public lectures and also taught yoga. Then he wrote his book of poems, *Song of The Soul* (Yogananda, 1983).

In 1924, he began lecturing in various US states. He spoke in front of thousands of people in many important cities. With the help of his disciples, at the end of 1925, he founded a new organization in Los Angeles. Over the years, he has spoken to hundreds of colleges, churches, clubs, and groups with diverse views. Between 1920 and 1930, his disciples in American yoga classes reached tens of thousands. In 1929 he gave them his new book, *Whispers from Eternity* (Yogananda, 2008).

Before returning to India in 1935, Yogananda registered the Self-Realization Fellowship (SRF) as an indefinite non-profit, non-sectarian center under California government law. He also granted the center all assets, including publishing all his works.

After staying in India for a while, he returned to the United States. Before the United States, he stayed in the United Kingdom for a few weeks, where he also preached the message of yoga. According to Yogananda, England also quickly adopted the yoga method. The disciples of the London Yoga Class formed the center for the SRF, where meditation was performed regularly, even during the war years (Neumann, 2019).

In 1942 he founded a center of SRF in Hollywood, and in 1947 established two centers in San Diego and Long Beach, California. In the 1950s and 1951s, he spent most of his time in California translating and commenting on the *Bhagavad Gita* (Neumann, 2019).

One of the most influential organizations that Yogananda founded was SRF in 1920 in Los Angeles, California. The group teaches kriya yoga. The association oversees all temples, meditation centers, and solitary confinement associations. The center has a global prayer circle that prays for all the physically and mentally ill and for world peace and harmony. The association is based in Los Angeles and includes several temples in other parts of California and Phoenix, Arizona, and facilities throughout the United States. This organization is also established in India as the Yogada Satsanga Society of India (Neumann, 2019).

More Details about Self-Realization Fellowship (SRF)

Self-Realization Fellowship (SRF) is a spiritual organization for offering Paramahamsa Yogananda teaching to people around the world. It was established in 1920 in Los Angeles to help people discover peace and divinity. The monks have accepted sacred in Kriya Yoga and are Paramahamsa Yogananda disciples.

Goals: The SRF organization was established with some goals such as:

To Spread knowledge for connecting God among different people around the world

To teach people the ultimate aim of life with self-realization and making temples worldwide

To point out that all religions and beliefs reach the divine way, which is the main way and scientific meditation

To liberate people from the three pains; physical sickness, inharmonic soul, and neglected soul

To encourage people toward simple life and deep thoughts and teach them to build a close relationship with God

To show people the priority of mind over the body and the soul over the mind

To overcome the mischief with righteousness, grief with happiness, cruelty with kindness, and ignorance with knowledge

To unify knowledge and religion.

To support the cultural unity between east and west

To teach people the importance of meditation, realizing death, creating spiritual relations, and teaching the ways of having a peaceful world for each person (Self-Realization Fellowship, n.d.)

Events: SRF activities and events are as follows:

The monks travel to different countries every year to spread Yogananda's teachings and help people know themselves. They hold classes as *How to Live*, and they hold group meditations.

They hold tours for new members to guide them and teach them their unique techniques.

Having programs for youth such as: holding classes for teens in summer in the country, holding meditation sessions to find their inner energy and make their life decisions based on them, holding trips to meditation gardens where Yogananda lived there for years, and meditating. They also built a heater, music room, laboratory, particular roads for hiking, basketball, and football field.

They hold a Parent Day when they meditate and visit the SRF gardens and their children.

The members can spend their time in Hidden Valley Ashram, where the environment is soothing, and they can choose their favorite place to connect with God and relax. They also join group meditation and use the swimming pool, library, and gym.

The SRF offers online services to gather people online and meditate and learn Jesus' instructions for those who cannot join the events (Self-Realization Fellowship, n.d.).

Another organization he founded is the *World Brotherhood Colonies*. The organization was Yogananda's idea for cooperation and assistance in spiritual life, which began in 1932 and continued until 1952. Yogananda encouraged American youth to raise funds, buy land, and form spiritual associations. He sought to establish the World Brotherhood Colonies in Southern California. In 1968, *Swami Kriyananda*, a direct disciple of Yogananda, founded the first *Ananda World Brotherhood Colonies*[5](Neumann, 2019).

Death

Yogananda was single for the rest of his life. He says of his decision: The single man thinks about God and how to seek the pleasure of God. A married person thinks about worldly affairs and making his wife happy. I had analyzed the lives of many of my friends who were married after particular spiritual disciplines, immersed in worldly responsibilities, and had forgotten their determination to meditate deeply. It was inconceivable to make God my second priority in life because he is the sole owner of the universe (Yogananda, 1982).

No details are available about the death of Yogananda and how he ended his life, but what is clear is that he died in 1952 in Los Angeles.

Books of Paramahamsa Yogananda

Yogananda leaves many books and articles, and as mentioned earlier, the SRF has collected and published all of his lectures. Nevertheless, some of his most important books are:

1. *Autobiography of Yogi:* This book has 49 chapters and contains information about Yogananda's life and thoughts. Among his memoirs, he also introduces the main concepts of yoga in this book.
2. *Man's Eternal Quest:* This book collects Yogananda lectures at temples or SRF centers. The book has also been published in two volumes, the second volume introducing the principles of SRF.
3. *Where There Is Light: Insight and Inspiration for Meeting Life's Challenges:* The book is written in 13 chapters, which teaches the principles of living calmly and communicating with others.
4. *The Divine Romance:* This book is also a collection of Yogananda teachings
5. *Spiritual Diary: An Each Day:* This book is a collection of Yogananda sayings in which the teachings of each day of the year are listed as a calendar.

Teachings and beliefs of Paramahamsa Yogananda

Science without mysticism is useless: Yogananda believes that science is useless without mysticism and without meditation. Because this science is used only for material life, everything, including science, must be used to achieve the ultimate goal of life, which is to reach God. He also considered Kiria Yoga as a means to reach God. For this purpose, in the schools he founded, he taught students a combination of science and Krya Yoga (Yogananda, 1982).

The need for self-awareness to have a better society: Yogananda's other claim about his movement is the self-awareness to build a better society.

Yogananda believed that if a person knows himself, achieves inner peace and tranquility; he can have a healthy and peaceful life in society. If the people achieve self-awareness and inner peace, the idea of utopia will be realized. The purpose of meditation and inner peace is to know God. When we know God, we will see His manifestation in everything so we will not make mistakes (Yogananda, 2008).

God or the Almighty Cosmic Force: To understand the concept of God in Yogananda's thought, we examine one of his spiritual experiences.

Yogananda went to the master's empty living room in the morning. He wanted to meditate, but he could not concentrate at all. He heard the voice of Sri Yukteswar Giri: Mukunda! He thought to himself that master always makes me meditate. Now that he knows why I came to his room, he should not distract me. The master called out again, but he remained stubbornly silent. The third time he called, his voice was rebuked. He protested and roared: Master, I am meditating. Sri Yukteswar Giri said: I know how you meditate! With a disturbed mind. Come here soon. Sri Yukteswar Giri said in a kind tone: My child! The mountains could not grant you what you wanted. You will achieve your heart's desire.

After this event, a tremendous mystical joy appeared in his soul, and he felt that he was connected to God and had become fully aware of the universe. Yogananda wanted to bow to master in gratitude for the experience of cosmic consciousness he had long sought. However, the master told him: You should not get too intoxicated with ecstasy. You still have much work to do in the world. It is the cosmic force that actively maintains all forms and forces. It is beyond transcendence and beyond the vibration of the emerging worlds in a vacuum full of joy. Those who reach the truth on earth have a similar dual life. In contrast, they are doing their duty in the world, immersed in joyful bliss. God has created all human beings from his infinite joy, want the man to return to him finally (Yogananda, 1982).

Yukteswar taught that worldly pleasures bore man after a while. The desires of the world are endless. Man is never completely satisfied, so he goes from one goal to another. The other goal he seeks is God because only he can grant lasting happiness. Worldly desires with the promise of false happiness cannot replace the soul's joy. Because God is always an unpredictable joy, we never get tired of Him (Neumann, 2019).

As explained above, based on the teachings of his master, Yogananda believes that God is absolute happiness that manifests itself only in a state of absolute ecstasy and silence, so as long as man is captive to the material body and mind, this eternal happiness remains hidden.

Gods, manifestations of the Almighty God: In his description of God, Yogananda considers God to have various manifestations and claims that he has observed the truth in some of those manifestations. Describing these effects, he says: Just as Christ embodied the evil force in Satan, so the Indian *Rishis* embodied the Creator, Sustainer, and Destroyer in certain forms. The ancient Rishis gave these forces the titles of Brahma (Creator), Vishnu (Preserver), and Shiva (Destroyer). These three powers have been the embodied forms of the ultimate truth (Pokazanyeva, 2015).

Thus, Yogananda believes that God has various manifestations, but a single power rule over all powers behind these manifestations.

Ishwar is another manifestation of God that Yogananda says he experienced as a child. He says of his observation:

Shortly after the healing, I had received from the power of Lahiri Mahasaya's image, in the morning, as I sat on the bed, I fell into a profound dream and experienced a powerful spiritual observation. I asked: What is darkness behind closed eyes? Suddenly a dazzling light appeared in front of my eyes. The bodies of saints meditating in the caves of the mountains appeared like images from a movie. I asked loudly: Who are you? The answer came: We are Himalayan yogis. I said I want to go to the Himalayas and be like you! My view has disappeared. However, I still felt a glow that said to me: I am Ishwar, I am the light, I want to be one with you; as my inner joy diminished, I regained the lasting legacy of the consciousness of unity and deeply realized that he is eternal, the ever-fresh joy of this memory remained long after that day (Yogananda, 2005).

The universe is the manifestation of God: Yogananda believes that God is manifest in all phenomena of the universe and that a universe is a place where he reveals himself to man through his creatures. In this regard, Yogananda says: Because God is beautiful, He created beauty in flowers to be a sign of His beauty. The beauty and fragrance of flowers are intended to remind man not to forget God and seek God through the phenomena of existence. Therefore, reaching God is through understanding His manifestations in the universe. It can be inferred that God has only one purpose in hiding himself in the phenomena of existence; he wants humankind to seek him freely with his will (Pokazanyeva, 2015).

According to Yogananda, God has already imagined and designed the universe in his mind, and all things are in a way his imagination, to which God has given a particle of consciousness, and among these phenomena, human consciousness is more remarkable than other creatures. God has placed His intelligence in human beings. On the other hand, God has made the way of human evolution and growth gradual so that man can achieve evolution by contemplating the signs of God, knowing God, and admiring His power. In other words, reach God, who is the leading destination of human evolution (Yogananda, 1982).

Motives for God-seeking and worship: Yogananda summarizes the motive for seeking God in humans in the following cases.

1. Satisfaction of inner need and inner happiness
2. Search for a cause above all causes in the universe
3. Observing tact and order throughout the universe (Neumann, 2019).

Yogananda puts it this way: Humans developed medical science to cure suffering and disease, but how did man act to find God? In response to this question, he explains: The first genuine concept of God can be found in the ancient texts of the *Vedas*. In the Vedic hymns, eternal truths are presented (Yogananda, 1982).

The first Indian monks were ardent seekers of the spiritual path. They realized that without inner satisfaction, the happiness of material life would not last. Therefore, man is always suffering. Accordingly, Yogananda concludes that the first motive for seeking God, at least among Hindus, was liberation and the destruction of suffering. Yogananda states another reason for seeking God: Even in the West, theism flourished when people realized the law of cause and effect. One can make something by using a series of tools and instructions (principles). Therefore, it can be said that the whole universe of creation must be formed based on principles and beliefs. Therefore, according to the law of cause and effect, intelligent human beings concluded that there must be a causal cause (Yogananda, 2008).

Therefore, another reason for seeking God among human beings is the need for a higher cause than other causes.

Dimensions of human existence: The Lord has created 35 ideas as matrix of human. basically, the energy and essence of physics are these ideas, 19 out of the 35 ideas contain the 10 senses, five of them are the force of living, intellect, mind, feeling, ego and life. the rest of the ideas which are 16, turned to pure elements such as iron, calcium, phosphorus etc. these elements create the astral physic of life so first they should be named as components of physic and each of them have their special characteristics.

The physical body is the result of solid vibration and the astral body is the result of energy vibrations and mental vibrations. the casual body also is the result of pure vibrations and cosmic awareness. the physical body needs food, astral body needs energy willing and thought and casual body needs wisdom. In general, the soul has been trapped in these three bodies (Yogananda. 1952).

Death: In Yogananda view, death is beautiful. Death does not mean the end of life but is a part of life and is God's plan for the liberation of man. Yogananda considers the soul to be the central aspect of man, so death is the only death of the body. "Death teaches us not to trust in the body, but to trust in God," he says. Therefore, death is our friend, and we should not grieve over the death of our loved ones unnecessarily. It is selfish that we want them always to be close to us for our happiness and comfort. Instead, we should be glad that they have been called to free their souls to a newer and better place in other worlds (Yogananda, 2016).

Yogananda believes that since death is part of God's creation, God wants us to love and fear it as much as any other part of life. With this interpretation, there is no reason to be afraid because, in this sense, death is a smile again to the soul's eternal life. In other words, Yogananda says that death is the liberating meaning of life, during which the soul trapped in the form of the body is released and attains pure liberation (Yogananda, 2016).

Death, although it seems accidental, it is not accidental at all; death is righteousness, truth, and justice. While it looks pretty unjust, death is grace and kindness. Death depends on the truth of the law of destiny because the law of destiny is based on grace and kindness and leads us very steadfastly to wisdom and to find spiritual perfection; this is a definite law. Illness, accidents, weakness, and disability of aging do not occur voluntarily but in harmony and adaptation to time in the world. These are our past actions (Yogananda, 2016).

It should be noted that Yogananda view of destiny means destiny that is made and controlled by human beings themselves. It refers to the factors that human beings have activated in the past and are witnessing its impact on future lives. Therefore, although death is part of the general plan of God's creation, it is human beings who, by their actions, determine death again in the cycle of reincarnation or liberating death, so the fate of death can also be changed (Neumann, 2019)

Karma and Reincarnation: Yogananda accepts the concept of reincarnation and relates it to karma. Regarding reincarnation, he says that the concept of reincarnation is not limited to Eastern philosophy, but has been introduced as a fundamental truth in many ancient civilizations. The Christian church initially accepted the issue of reincarnation, an issue raised by mystics and some popes, including the priests of Alexandria, Origen, and St. Jerome. At the Second Council of Constantinople in 553 ADS, this doctrine was formally removed from the teachings of the Church. Today, some Western thinkers are turning to the law of karma and reincarnation, which is a justification for the apparent inequalities of life (Yogananda. 1982).

Yogananda says he recalls memories of his early years irregularly. He also has vivid memories of the life he lived as a yogi in the Himalayas. Of course, he emphasizes that the recollection of past lives is due to the existence of the soul in man, and if man were only a body, he would not have experienced any other lives at all. Explaining this theory, he says that how many yogis who have maintained their unbroken self-consciousness due to the abnormal transition from life to death, if man were only a body, his death would end his identity as well. But all the sages throughout the millennia have said that man is essentially a soul and not dependent on time (Yogananda. 2005).

Regarding the law of karma and its effect on reincarnation, he says: Karma is the effect of past actions on the present or future lives. The word is derived from the Sanskrit word Karman meaning to act. The law of equilibrium of karma is the law of action and reaction or cause and effect. In the path of justice of nature and existence, every human being shapes his destiny with his thoughts and actions. Any energy he moves wisely or irrationally must be returned to him. Understanding the law of karma as the law of justice frees the human mind from any resentment against God and the people. The karma of each person, from reincarnation to reincarnation, follows him until the person reaches complete spiritual balance.

According to these explanations, karma and the deeds that man does are the cause of rebirth, and man spends other lives, good or bad, according to past actions, this process continues until man can be freed from reincarnation and Reach balance. Explaining whether one can get rid of the effects of karma, Yogananda says that even the possessor of the worst karma, if he constantly thinks of the Absolute Truth, is freed from the effects of his past deeds and attains permanent peace (Yogananda. 1952).

Suffering and its cause: Yogananda believes that Maya is the deceptive power in the structure of creation by which unity manifests itself in multiplicity. Maya is the principle of relativity, inversion, contradiction, duality, the opposite of the devil, whom Jesus called a criminal and a liar; Because there is nothing right in it.

Yogananda refers to the Maya to explain the mechanism of miracles performed by some humans. Vedic texts say that the material world acts under the Maya law (principle of relativity and duality), while God is the only absolute unity; The unity that is hidden and manifested in multiplicity, which is the Maya. Newton's law of motion is the same as Maya's law. Every action always has an equal and reciprocal reaction. In this way action and reaction are always equal. Maya literally means a grand magical measurer (from the Sanskrit root ma, "to measure"). In fact, Maya is the magical power of creation (Yogananda. 2005).

How is the Maya the cause of suffering in humanity? Yogananda says that the Maya law, which is the hallucinatory principle of creation, causes suffering and draws people from unity to plurality due to the creation of contradictions and dualities in human life. It ultimately leads to suffering for unconscious human beings. Excess in sensual pleasures leads to satiety and disgust. The constant experience of these dichotomies makes people depressed and unreliable. Characteristic of the Maya or delusional state is the constant presence of these contrasting pairs (Yogananda. 1982).

Yogananda believes that God created the Maya at the same time as man was created, so that man can use the power of his will to find the path to happiness. Maya is the realm of divine testing in which every human being is tested. Suffering is caused by the misuse of the human will. God has given us the authority to accept or deny Him, and He does not want us to suffer. But it does not interfere when we choose actions that lead to suffering. Yogananda therefore describes man as the cause of suffering. Because by misusing the power of his will, he chooses the path of Maya and always suffers. In his view, as long as man is captivated by worldly illusions and lives in ignorance and stubbornness, the existence of suffering is inevitable. But man can end suffering by shifting his perception and will to God. Also, Yogananda considers desires as the basis of suffering. He says that desires are the cruelest enemies of man because he cannot suppress them. Have only one wish, knowing God, satisfying sensual desires cannot please you; Because you are not one with your senses; They are your only servants (Yogananda. 1982).

Freedom and liberation from suffering; The destination of spiritual conduct: As mentioned, the cause of suffering for Yogananda is desires and aspirations. And the reason why man suffers from them is that he considers plurals as the principle instead of the real unity. And it is the Maya who have the power of deception and delusion. Therefore, when man is free from desires and aspirations, he can discover the truth, and attain liberation. According to Yogananda, the end of human endeavors on the path to liberation is attaining the level of consciousness (Yogananda. 1952). From his point of view, consciousness has different states, which are explained below.The states of consciousness are divided into five categories:

A) Immortal consciousness: At this stage, man experiences three levels. Awakening consciousness, sleep consciousness and dream consciousness. The mortal man does not experience the soul and the subconscious. He does not experience God either; For the mortal man is conscious through the body, but the transcendent man is conscious through the universe which he feels as his body. Cosmic consciousness is beyond, that is, the experience of joining God in His absolute consciousness (Yogananda. 1982).

B) The consciousness of Christ: Christ or the consciousness of Christ is the manifested consciousness of the presence of God in all creation, which in the sacred texts of Christianity, it is called the only pure manifestation of God in creation. In Hindu scriptures it is also called Kutastha Chaitanya or Tat[6], which is manifested in all creation. This is universal awareness and union with God. Christ, Krishna and other avatars are symbols of this consciousness. The great mystics and yogis call it samadhi. At this stage, their consciousness is equated with the consciousness of all the particles of the universe. In this state, they feel the whole universe as their body (Yogananda. 1983).

C) Cosmic consciousness: This stage is also called the Absolute God and the soul beyond creation. Samadhi and union with God and Samadhi are in the same stage; A state that involves both the outside and the inside of the vibrating particles of the universe.

D) Super consciousness: Super consciousness is pure, intuitive and absolutely blessed to the soul. It is sometimes used to refer to all the different levels of communication with God that are experienced when meditating, but specifically, it refers to the first level of concentration in which man finds himself as a spirit and a manifestation of God (Yogananda. 1952).

E) Self-realization: Self-realization means knowing physically, mentally and spiritually that God is present and witnessing everywhere. And we are one with him and we belong to him. Self-realization means that we should not pray to God to come to us because we are not only close to Him all the time, but the fact that He is everywhere means we are everywhere and we are as much a part of Him as we will be in the future. All we have to do is increase our knowledge (Yogananda. 2005).

Therefore, the highest level that every human being can achieve in life is the level of self-fulfillment, that is, when human beings find themselves with God and in God at all times. In fact, these states should become permanent for him and come out of temporary states.

How can liberation be achieved?

Yogananda has stated the means of attaining liberation and reaching the absolute reality of the universe in the following cases:

Denial of ego and abandonment of worldly belongings: According to Yogananda, the highest enemy in knowing God is the ego. Because he gets tired soon and wants to give up everything. This is where purifying the ego helps one to overcome one's material belongings. The most important thing is that man lives in this world far from selfishness. It does not matter if he believes in reincarnation or not. In any case, his view of life must be to please God. In the way of gaining divine knowledge, denying the ego equals the first step of ascension. Because as long as there is an ego and its desires, it is not possible to know God. Explaining the concept of self-denial, Yogananda says that self-denial does not mean giving up everything, but means giving up temporary pleasures for the sake of eternal bliss. Therefore, self-denial is not an end in itself, but a means to an end (Yogananda. 2008).

Sincere and continuous prayer: Yogananda emphasizes the non-worship of God Almighty. He says that if you really want to know God, you must pray to Him and insist on your prayers enough. If a person reaches a correct understanding of God, then he will not get tired of praying to God and will insist on his prayers every day. It should be known that not every prayer is acceptable to God, the prayer in which the soul burns with the desire of God, is the only prayer that is effective. Man must speak to God eagerly; in which case the prayer will be answered. Yogananda emphasizes that God is very close and it is enough for human beings to want him, in which case he reveals himself to his servant's heart. Therefore, according to Yogananda, with the right action and sincere worship of God, God is revealed, it is enough to take one step towards him so that God takes ten more steps. Of course, sincere prayer requires a pure and honest heart and mind, which is why Yogananda emphasizes self-improvement before prayer (Yogananda. 1983).

Meditation and yoga: One of the most important ways to help awaken inner feelings from Yogananda point of view is through yoga or meditation. Regarding the word yoga, he says that yoga comes from the Sanskrit word Yui meaning connection. Yoga means the techniques through which unity is achieved; the techniques of yoga are different. The part that is taught in the course of self-fulfilling prophecy is Raja Yoga, taught by Bhagavan Krishna at the Bhagavad Gita. Patanjali, the first and oldest yoga teacher, introduced eight steps to yoga:

1- Yama (moral behavior)
2- Niyama (performing religious duties)
3- Asana (correct physical condition)
4- Pranayama (control of prana or subtle currents of life)
5- Pratyahara (introspection)
6- Dharana (focus)
7- Dhyana (meditation)
8- Samadhi (super conscious experience).

In his descriptions, Yogananda considers yoga to be a science for all people, anytime, anywhere. He believes that yoga is a way to calm thoughts. Because the mind does not allow man to realize his true and infinite nature. For this reason, he believes that there is a big difference between a monk and a yogi, because a monk has formally joined the order of leaving the world, while a yogi is someone who uses one of the scientific techniques to reach God. Thus, a yogi can be single or married, or have worldly responsibilities, or even be bound by one of the official rituals. The monk may be leaving the world. But the yogi takes a step-by-step approach that trains his body and mind so that his soul can be gradually liberated (Yogananda. 1982).

Yogananda distinguishes yoga from strenuous austerities or grueling practical exercises. According to him, a good yogi is one who has the ability to control his body and mind and take control of his soul.

In addition, Yogananda was more inclined to Kriya Yoga. The Sanskrit root Kri means To Do. As a result, kriya yoga means connection with God through performing certain acts or rituals or kriya. A person who uses this technique regularly will gradually get rid of karma. According to Yogananda, kriya yoga is a sacred divine knowledge that began thousands of years ago in India. kriya is a form of Raja Yoga that is worshiped by Krishna at the Bhagavad Gita. Kriya Yoga was revived in the present age by Mahavatar Babaji. Yogananda claims that Babaji chose him to spread this knowledge around the world and pass it on to future generations in the same special way.

Love: One way to reach absolute truth, according to Yogananda, is to cultivate love within man. Although his statements in this regard are very brief. He says that divine love is indescribable, but when the human heart is refined and calmed, this love can be felt. When the mind and senses realize the inside, a person feels the divine joy, the pleasures of the five senses do not last, but the divine joy is eternal and unique. In other words, divine love requires self-liberation.

Liberation is the way to God, without God's love, human love is not complete. Worldly love is selfishness, selfishness rooted in desires. True love branches out from God. Only people who have purified their hearts can understand the love of God. In other words, the feelings of the heart are the channels through which people can understand God. The path of love in the path of liberation and attainment of the transcendent truth is the best way to understand the absolute truth of existence, and this is not possible except through intuition. Intuition is not possible except by self-improvement and liberation from the prison of the mind. Therefore, what is considered important for Yogananda is the replacement of divine love in the human heart with worldly and temporary love. Divine love has everything else with it, it evokes happiness that cannot be found anywhere (Yogananda. 1952).

Similarities Between beliefs of Yogananda and Teachings of Islam

Yogananda sought more harmony between Christianity (the original teachings of Jesus), Hinduism, and the yoga method and paid less attention to other religions. However, he respected all religions, and he followed his masters in this regard. He ignored the caste system and other social discrimination, just like his masters (Self-Realization Fellowship, 2021).

Nevertheless, Yogananda felt that the essence of all religions, also known as Sanatan Dharma, was equal and that everyone had a common goal. Moreover, anyone from any religion can achieve the primary goal of creation.

Yogananda also has a poem in one of his books about the Prophet of Islam, Muhammad, called Muhammad, Come to Me. This poem is part of a prayer, and it says that you can meditate with prayer and reach God.

In addition, he has written commentaries on the poems of Omar Khayyam, a Muslim mystic, and acknowledges that Omar Khayyam is a unique Muslim mystic (Self-Realization Fellowship, 2021).

However, similarities can be found between his beliefs and the verses of the Qur'an. for example:

Self-awareness as a prerequisite for knowing God: As mentioned, Yogananda sees self-awareness as a prerequisite for knowing God, having a better society, peace, and reaching God. In this regard, God says in the Qur'an: " Do not be like those who forget Allah, so He makes them forget their own souls. It is they who are the transgressors (Quran 19:59 Universal

Unity edition)[7]." Another example is: "Certainly We have created man, and We know to what his soul tempts him, and We are nearer to him than his jugular vein (Quran 16:50 Universal Unity edition)[8]." "When My servants ask you about Me, [tell them that] I am indeed nearmost. I answer the supplicant's call when he calls Me. So let them respond to Me, and let them have faith in Me, so that they may fare rightly (Quran 186:1 Universal Unity edition)[9]."

Manifestation of God in all beings: In the Qur'an, there are many verses about achieving theology through the contemplation of creatures, for instance: "It is He who made the sun a radiance and the moon a light, and ordained its phases that you might know the number of years and the calculation [of time]. Allah did not create all that except with justice. He elaborates the signs for a people who have knowledge (Quran 5:10 Universal Unity edition)[10]", And "Indeed in the alternation of night and day, and whatever Allah has created in the heavens and the earth, there are surely signs for a people who are Godwary (Quran 6:10 Universal Unity edition)[11]." There are also many verses in the Quran about God being omnipresent: "To Allah belong the east and the west: so whichever way you turn, there is the face of Allah! Allah is indeed all-bounteous, all-knowing (Quran 115:1 Universal Unity edition)[12]", "It is He who created the heavens and the earth in six days; then settled on the Throne. He knows whatever enters the earth and whatever emerges from it and whatever descends from the sky and whatever ascends to it, and He is with you wherever you may be, and Allah watches what you do (Quran 57:4 Universal Unity edition)[13]."

Conclusion of Chapter

In this chapter, the author describes the movement presented by Paramahamsa Yogananda and examines the similarities between this movement and Islamic teachings. However, no definite opinion can be given as to whether or not the teachings of Islam affect Yogananda. As mentioned earlier, Yogananda knew his mission was to invite the West to yoga and the ideas of Hinduism, so naturally, he had to use the teachings of Christianity and the religions prevalent in the West to explain his ideas.

[1] Shyama Charan Lahiri, best known as Lahiri Mahasaya, was an Indian yogi, guru

[2] Sri Yukteswar Giri is the monastic name of Priya Nath Karar, an Indian monk and yogi, and the guru of Paramahansa Yogananda

[3] The traditional color of monks' clothing in India

[4] A city in Bihar

[5] Ananda Village was founded by Swami Kriyananda and a handful of young friends in 1968 on 70 acres of land in the Sierra Nevada foothills of California. The fledgling community was initially faced with many tests and challenges: lack of money, the threat of foreclosure, a devastating fire that destroyed most of the existing structures, differing ideas about the community's purpose–but in the end, all seeming hardships served to help forge a community dedicated to living Yogananda's ideal of putting God first, in all circumstances.

[6] the cosmic consciousness of the soul

[7] آیه 19 سوره مبارکه حشر: وَلَا تَكُونُوا كَالَّذِينَ نَسُوا اللَّهَ فَأَنْسَاهُمْ أَنْفُسَهُمْ ۚ أُولَٰئِكَ هُمُ الْفَاسِقُونَ

[8] آیه 16 سوره مبارکه ق: وَلَقَدْ خَلَقْنَا الْإِنْسَانَ وَنَعْلَمُ مَا تُوَسْوِسُ بِهِ نَفْسُهُ ۖ وَنَحْنُ أَقْرَبُ إِلَيْهِ مِنْ حَبْلِ
الْوَرِيدِ

[9] آیه 186 سوره مبارکه بقره: وَإِذَا سَأَلَكَ عِبَادِي عَنِّي فَإِنِّي قَرِيبٌ ۖ أُجِيبُ دَعْوَةَ الدَّاعِ إِذَا دَعَانِ ۖ
فَلْيَسْتَجِيبُوا لِي وَلْيُؤْمِنُوا بِي لَعَلَّهُمْ يَرْشُدُونَ

[10] آیه 5 سوره مبارکه یونس: هُوَ الَّذِي جَعَلَ الشَّمْسَ ضِيَاءً وَالْقَمَرَ نُورًا وَقَدَّرَهُ مَنَازِلَ لِتَعْلَمُوا عَدَدَ
السِّنِينَ وَالْحِسَابَ ۚ مَا خَلَقَ اللَّهُ ذَٰلِكَ إِلَّا بِالْحَقِّ ۚ يُفَصِّلُ الْآيَاتِ لِقَوْمٍ يَعْلَمُونَ

[11] آیه 6 سوره مبارکه یونس: إِنَّ فِي اخْتِلَافِ اللَّيْلِ وَالنَّهَارِ وَمَا خَلَقَ اللَّهُ فِي السَّمَاوَاتِ وَالْأَرْضِ لَآيَاتٍ
لِقَوْمٍ يَتَّقُونَ

[12] آیه 115 سوره مبارکه بقره: وَلِلَّهِ الْمَشْرِقُ وَالْمَغْرِبُ ۚ فَأَيْنَمَا تُوَلُّوا فَثَمَّ وَجْهُ اللَّهِ ۚ إِنَّ اللَّهَ وَاسِعٌ عَلِيمٌ

[13] آیه 4 سوره مبارکه حدید: هُوَ الَّذِي خَلَقَ السَّمَاوَاتِ وَالْأَرْضَ فِي سِتَّةِ أَيَّامٍ ثُمَّ اسْتَوَىٰ عَلَى الْعَرْشِ ۚ
يَعْلَمُ مَا يَلِجُ فِي الْأَرْضِ وَمَا يَخْرُجُ مِنْهَا وَمَا يَنْزِلُ مِنَ السَّمَاءِ وَمَا يَعْرُجُ فِيهَا ۖ وَهُوَ مَعَكُمْ أَيْنَ مَا كُنْتُمْ ۚ وَاللَّهُ بِمَا
تَعْمَلُونَ بَصِيرٌ

V
Conclusion

The study of India's cultural, social, and religious issues has always been one of the topics of interest for researchers. In this study, the author has tried to investigate the issue of Hindu religious, social movements in modern India. Based on this, two case studies were selected, Ramakrishna Mission and Paramahamsa Yogananda.

Before explaining any case studies, it is better to answer the first research question about the characteristics of socio-religious reform movements in modern India.

What are the main features of socio-religious reforms movements in India?

To better understand this issue, we first discuss the general characteristics of reform movements:

1. At the heart of any reform movement is the pursuit of building a better society.
2. One of the influential components in reform movements is religious beliefs. Also, Wilkinson (1971) describes reform movements as "emergencies" or "sub-movements" of more significant religious movements.
3. As a means of planned and directed changes, the reform movement often attracts the educated and intelligentsia of the middle class.

Prior to the nineteenth century, Hinduism had stagnated and been distorted by the rise of Islam in the Indian subcontinent. However, in the nineteenth century, with the advent of British colonialism, the stagnation and distortion of Hinduism became more apparent. Due to the presence of Christian missionaries in India and the propagation of Christianity, British criticism of Hindu savage customs such as Sati and caste, modern British education for Indian youth, including middle-class education, and the presence of orientalists in India to study Indian culture and tradition. Indian thinkers thought of reforming Hinduism. The first leader of the modern Hindu movements was Raja Ram Mohan Roy. The reasons given were one of the main factors in the formation of reform movements in modern India, which took place in four periods:

1. The 1800s to 1828s: This period can be considered a beginning of awareness of the need for change and reform in Hinduism. As well, it is the period of preparation for the movement.
2. 1828 to 1870: This period was the beginning of the reform movement, which was more in defense of Hinduism against the British-induced culture. People such as Raja Ram Mohan Roy and the Brahmo Samaj organization also tried to reform the violent traditions of Hinduism, such as Sati.
3. 1870 to 1900: This period of reform is a time of defending the ideologies of Hinduism and returning to the original texts of this religion, namely the Vedas and the Gita. Great mystics and thinkers such as Ramakrishna and Vivekananda emerged during this period.
4. From 1900 onwards: This period can be considered the evolution of the philosophical and political system, the struggle for independence, and the growth of reform movements, including those that emphasized yoga and self-awareness, such as the Yogananda movement.

Another critical point is about the approach and characteristics of the nineteenth-century reform movements. The approach of modern reform movements was quite different from that of the past. New movements, for example, are a combination of Western methods and Eastern content.

Other differences of the modern reform movement can be seen in the following:

Attention to society and the growth of society instead of mere attention to the individual

Re-interpret the sacred texts of the Vedas, Upanishads, and Gita and dispel their superstitions

Having a monotheistic approach instead of polytheism

Establish connections with other religions and avoid restricting Hinduism

Emphasis on the reality of Hinduism instead of complicated and incorrect religious rites

What are the main reforms introduced by Ramakrishna Mission?

As mentioned, one of the case studies in this study is Ramakrishna Mission, which the author tried to answer the research question in this regard.

Mission Ramakrishna (RKM) is a Hindu religious and spiritual organization that has launched a global movement called the Ramakrishna Movement or the Vedanta Movement. The original idea for the movement and its name was inspired by the great Indian mystic Ramakrishna, founded on May 1, 1897, by his chief disciple, Swami Vivekananda.

In addition to religious and spiritual education, the organization carries out extensive educational and humanitarian activities in India and abroad. This aspect was a feature of many Hindu movements. Ramakrishna's mission is centered worldwide and publishes many critical Hindu texts. The teachings of this movement are based on the thoughts, ideas, and teachings of Ramakrishna and, later, his disciple, Vivekananda.

Regarding Ramakrishna's beliefs, it should be emphasized that since he had experienced mysticism in almost all religions, including Islam, his principles and beliefs were also inspired by various religions. The same ideas were developed by Vivekananda and followed in the Ramakrishna Mission. These ideas are:

God-realization is the ultimate goal of life because all existence belongs to God, and creatures are only manifestations of God.

Harmony of Religions: It is stated in the Vedas that different names know ultimate reality. The Gita also said that different spiritual paths lead to the same destination. Using these two propositions, Ramakrishna proved that all religions pursue the same goal and that all religions in the world are equal.

The human soul originates from Brahman, our innate happiness is due to Brahman, and if one turns to worldly life, it is ignorance. If ignorance reduces, the human soul will be closer to Brahman.

The way to get rid of ignorance and suffering and reach God is yoga.

Working in any job is sacred. Serving the people means worshiping God, and this service should create the well-being of the poor.

What are the main reforms introduced by Paramahamsa Yogananda?

Another case study is about the Paramahamsa Yogananda movement. Among the influential points in choosing this movement is its newness, focus on the development of yoga and the teachings of Hinduism in America and Europe and gradually other countries of the world, and striving for self-awareness as an essential step for having a better society.

Yogananda claimed that to have a better society, to achieve world peace, man must strive for self-awareness, know himself, and strengthen his spiritual connection with God. According to Yogananda, these goals can be achieved through Kriya Yoga. Yogananda also believed that academic science acquired through the university was useless. Science is used when it is combined with yoga and meditation.

For this purpose, he gave hundreds of lectures at universities, seminars, and temples, all of which tried to scientifically prove the value and importance of yoga and meditation and the mystical concepts, theology, and the ultimate purpose of life. Additionally, Yogananda registered many centers and organizations, like the Self-Realization Fellowship (SRF) and the World Brotherhood Colonies. The main and most extensive of these centers is the SRF, with over 500 branches in the United States, Europe, and other countries. Also, SRF works in India as Yogoda Satsanga Society of India (YSS). The goals of these organizations, including the SRF, are to teach Yogananda beliefs and invite people to meditate and learn the method of self-awareness, regardless of social class, religion, or race.

Yogananda's beliefs include the following:

God is absolute happiness that manifests itself only in a state of absolute ecstasy and silence, so as long as man is captive to the material body and mind, this eternal happiness remains hidden.

God has various manifestations and claims that he has observed the truth in some of those manifestations. Also, all the gods that people know are the manifestation of absolute power.

God is manifest in all phenomena of the universe, and a universe is a place where he reveals himself to man through his creatures.

What is the relationship between the modern Hindu reforms and teachings of Islam?

Another point in this section is the relationship between Islamic teachings and socio-religious reform movements in modern India.

In general, Islam has played a significant role in forming reform movements in India, both the first reform movements in the fifteenth century and the reform movements in modern India in the nineteenth century.

For finding the answer to the above question, historical evidence was examined. Islam entered the Indian subcontinent in the 7th century AD with the conquest of Indus by the Arabs, and later reached northern India through the conquest of the Ghurids in the 12th century, and has since become part of Indian culture and history.

The beginning of Muslim rule in the subcontinent is considered after the twelfth century AD.

There are several main reasons for the spread of Islam in the Indian subcontinent:

The rule of Muslim kings and the establishment of Islamic law in those kingdoms led to the people becoming acquainted with Islam.

Distortions in the original teachings of Hinduism that resulted from the monopoly of sacred texts by the Brahmins, for example, after the Vedic period, the cassette system gradually changed, and living conditions became much more difficult for the lower castes and Dalits. Hence, to escape the harsh conditions of the caste system, they converted to other religions such as Jainism, Islam, and Buddhism. It can be concluded that those who converted to other religions such as Islam and became acquainted with these religions were better able to understand the discrimination in the Hindu system.

Another reason is the scattering of Muslims throughout the Indian subcontinent, even in areas under Hindu rule. It can even be said that Muslim mystics were more influential in the formation of Hindu reform movements because after examining the Hindu reform movements in the fourteenth to sixteenth centuries, we find that Islam and Muslim mystics directly inspired their leaders. For example, one of the great religious leaders whose works show the undeniable influence of Islam is Guru Nanak (1469-1539). The Sikh religion, founded by Nanak, is distinct from its anti-Islamic faction but is essentially the seventeenth-century historical context. Nanak's goal was to unite Hindus and Islam by appealing to what they both consider to be fundamental truths. He considers Kabir (one of the great Muslim mystics) as his spiritual teacher, and their teachings are very similar. His debt to Islam is expressed in his emphasis on the will and greatness of God, while the basic structure of thought, with a desire for complete unity, reflects his Hindu heritage.

On the other hand, Ramakrishna has been a Muslim for some time and claims to have experienced high levels of Islamic mysticism, so he is fully acquainted with Islam. His chief disciple, Vivekananda, and his family also had close ties to Muslim mystics and thinkers, and as noted in Vivekananda's memoirs, his father was interested in the social laws of Islam. In addition, there are many similarities between Ramakrishna's beliefs and the teachings of Islam, such as verses of the Quran and hadiths, that are mentioned in chapter 3. Thus, concerning the Ramakrishna movement, it can be said that the teachings of Islam influenced him.

Regarding the Yogananda movement, it is not possible to say with certainty whether the teachings of Islam influenced him or not. However, according to what he has stated, he knew the Muslim mystics, the Prophet of Islam and its laws, and he also mentions Omar Khayyam as the most significant Muslim mystic and is interested in his thoughts.

References

Akram, M. (2017). God-Realisation through Multiple Religions? A Study into Religious Experiences of Sri Ramakrishna. *Islamic Studies, 56*(1-2), 31-52.

Altıntaş, İ. (2017). *Revivalist discourse in modern hinduism: a socio-religious study of the ramakrishna movement* (Master's thesis, İbn Haldun Üniversitesi, Medeniyetler İttifakı Enstitüsü).

Anjum, T. (2007). The Emergence of Muslim Rule in India: Some Historical Disconnects and Missing Links. Islamic studies, 217-240.

Aurobindo, S. (1999). *The ideal of human unity*. Lotus Press.

Avalon, A. (1914). *Principles of Tantra.[Edited by A. Avalon.]*. Luzac & Company.

Beckerlegge, G. (2000). *The Ramakrishna Mission: The making of a modern Hindu movement*. Oxford University Press.

Beckford, J. A. (1986). *New religious movements and rapid social change.* Sage.

Bottomore, T. B. (1962). Sociology in India. The British Journal of Sociology, 13(2), 98-106.

Chandra, S. (1998). Encyclopaedia of Hindu gods and goddesses. Sarup & Sons.

Christiansen, J. (2009). Four stages of social movements. *EBSCO Research Starters, 1248.*

Copland, I. (2006). Christianity as an arm of empire: The ambiguous case of India under the Company, c. 1813-1858. *Historical Journal*, 1025-1054.

Davis, R. H. (2014). *The Bhagavad Gita*. Princeton University Press.

Deshpande, M. S. (2010). *History of the Indian caste system and its impact on India today*. Digital Commons.

Deshpande, M. S. (2010). History of the Indian caste system and its impact on India today.

Deshpande, M. S. (2010). History of the Indian caste system and its impact on India today.

Doniger, W. (2018, September 11). Bhagavadgita. Encyclopedia Britannica. https://www.britannica.com/topic/Bhagavadgita

Doniger, W. , Basham, . Arthur Llewellyn , Dimock, . Edward C. , Smith, . Brian K. , Gold, . Ann G. , Buitenen, . J.A.B. van and Narayanan, . Vasudha (2020, November 30). Hinduism. Encyclopedia Britannica. https://www.britannica.com/topic/Hinduism

D'Souza, G. (2001). Spiritual theology in Indian thought. *Teresianum: Rivista della Pontificia Facoltà Teologica e del Pontificio Istituto di Spiritualità" Teresianum"*, 52(1), 357-379.

Elangovan, A. (2017). Social Movements in India, 1800 to the Present. In *The History of Social Movements in Global Perspective* (pp. 265-295). Palgrave Macmillan, London.

Farquhar, J. N. (1977). *Modern Religious Movements in India*, reprint ed. Munshiram Manoharlal.

Fosse, L. M. (2007). *The Bhagavad Gita: the original Sanskrit and an English translation*. YogaVidya. com.

Frauwallner, E. (1973). History of Indian Philosophy: The philosophy of the Veda and of the epic. The Buddha and the Jina. The Sāmkhya and the classical Yoga-system (Vol. 1). Motilal Banarsidass Publishe.

Frauwallner, E. (1973). *History of Indian Philosophy: The philosophy of the Veda and of the epic. The Buddha and the Jina. The Sāmkhya and the classical Yoga-system* (Vol. 1). Motilal Banarsidass Publishe.

Frykenberg, R. E. (Ed.). (2013). *Christians and missionaries in India: Cross-cultural communication since 1500*. Routledge.

Ghose, S. (2003). The dalit in India. Social Research: An International Quarterly, 70(1), 83-109.

Gokhale, B. G. (1965). *Muslim Civilization in India. By SM Ikram*. Edited by Ainslie T. Embree.(New York: Columbia University Press. 1964. Pp. x, 325. $6.00.).

Gyan, P. A. (2000). *An analysis of the pedagogical methods of Hindu gurus (Ramakrishna, Ramana Maharshi, Paramahamsa Yogananda).* University of San Diego

Haldar, H. (2018). Realistic idealism. *In Contemporary Indian philosophy* (pp. 213-232). Routledge.

Jackson, C. T. (1994). *Vedanta for the West: The Ramakrishna Movement in the United States.* Indiana University Press.

Jha, G. (2003). *Yoga-Darshana: Sutras of Patanjali With Bhasya of Vyasa.* Asian Humanities Press

Jones, K. W. (1989). *Socio-religious reform movements in British India* (Vol. 1). Cambridge University Press.

Kalupahana, D. J. (1972). Bhikshu Sangharakshita, THE THREE JEWELS: AN INTRODUCTION TO MODERN BUDDHISM (Book Review). Philosophy East and West, 22(2), 227.Kaur, T. (2015). Role of Arya Samaj in Propagation of Vedic Religion. *Asian Journal of Research in Social Sciences and Humanities,*

5(7), 110-115.

Kopf, D. (2015). *The Brahmo Samaj and the shaping of the modern Indian mind*. Princeton University Press.

Lal, B. K. (1978). *Contemporary Indian Philosophy*. Motilal Banarsidass Publ..

Levinson, D., & Ember, M. (Eds.). (1996). Encyclopedia of cultural anthropology (Vol. 4). New York: Holt.

Macdonell, A. A. (2004). *A practical Sanskrit dictionary with transliteration, accentuation, and etymological analysis throughout*. Motilal Banarsidass Publ..

Majumdar, R. C. (1977). *Ancient India*. Motilal Banarsidass Publ..

Malhotra, A. K. (2017). *An Introduction to Yoga Philosophy: an annotated translation of the Yoga Sutras*. Routledge.

Mandal, M. M. M., & Behera, S. K. (2015). raja ram Mohan roy as an Educational reformer: an Evaluation. *International Journal of Humanities & Social Science Studies*.

Masson-Ousel, P., Stern, P., & Willman-Grabowska, H. (2013). Ancient India and Indian Civilization. Routledge.

Medhananda, S. (2020). Was swami vivekananda a hindu supremacist? revisiting a long-standing debate. *Religions*, 11(7), 368. doi:http://dx.doi.org/10.3390/rel11070368

Mehrotra, R. (2011). *Thakur-Sri Ramakrishna: A Biography*. Hay House, Inc.

Michaels, A. (2004). *Hinduism: past and present*. Princeton University Press.

Miller, D. (1999). Modernity in Hindu Monasticism:· Swami Vivekananda and the Ramakrishna Movement. *Journal of Asian and African Studies, 34*(1), 111-126.

Mishra, K. (1981). *Significance of the Tantric tradition*. Arddhanarisvara Publications.

Muller, F. M. (1899). *Ramakrishna: His life and sayings*. Scribner.

Neumann, D. J. (2016). *Yogi Evangelist: Swami Yogananda's Mission to Modern America* (Doctoral dissertation, University of Southern California).

Neumann, D. J. (2019). *Finding god through yoga: Paramahamsa Yogananda and modern American religion in a global age*. UNC Press Books.

Nikhilananda, S. (1953). *Vivekananda: A biography*. Advaita Ashrama (A publication branch of Ramakrishna Math, Belur Math).

Parpola, A. (2015). The roots of Hinduism: the early Aryans and the Indus civilization. Oxford University Press, USA.

Powell, A. A. (2010). *Scottish Orientalists and India: The Muir Brothers, Religion, Education and Empire* (Vol. 4). Boydell & Brewer.

Radhakrishnan, S. (1940). *Eastern religions and western thought.* Oxford University Press, London.

Radhakrishnan, S., & Radhakrishnan, S. (1929). *Indian philosophy* (Vol. 2). London: Allen & Unwin.

Ramakrishna Math and Ramakrishna Mission. (2021, Sep, 13). *Highlights Of The Year 2019-20.* https://media.belurmath.org/highlights-of-the-year-2019-20-7637/

Ramakrishna Math and Ramakrishna Mission. (n.d.). *Emblem.* https://belurmath.org/emblem/

Ramakrishna Math and Ramakrishna Mission. (n.d.). *Ideology.* https://belurmath.org/ideology/

Ramakrishna Math and Ramakrishna Mission. (n.d.). *Service as a Way of Life – Key Features and Activities.* https://belurmath.org/activities/

Richards, J. F. (1995). The Mughal Empire (Vol. 5). Cambridge University Press.

Richter, J. (1908). *A history of missions in India* (Vol. 60). Oliphant.

Rolland, R. (1929). A great Indian mystic: Ramakrishna. *Europe , 19* (74), 153.

Rolland, R. (1929). *Ramakrishna's life.* Advaita Ashram.

Rolland, R. (1997). *The life of Vivekananda.* Prabhat Prakashan.

Self-Realization Fellowship. (n.d.). *Aims and Ideals.* https://yogananda.org/aims-and-ideals

Self-Realization Fellowship. (n.d.). *programs for youth.* https://yogananda.org/events-and-programs-for-youth

Shah, M. (2008). Structures of power in Indian Society: a response. *Economic and Political Weekly*, 78-83.

Shamsuddin, M. (2020). A brief historical background of Sati tradition in India. *Din ve Felsefe Araştırmaları*, 3(5), 44-63.

Sharma, A. (Ed.). (1988). *Neo-Hindu Views of Christianity.* Brill.

Shilling, C., & Mellor, P. A. (2011). Retheorising Emile Durkheim on society and religion: embodiment, intoxication and collective life. *The Sociological Review*, *59*(1), 17-41.

Smith, G. (2011). *The Life of William Carey, DD: Shoemaker and Missionary.* Cambridge University Press.

Srivastava, R. S. (1965). *Contemporary Indian Philosophy*. Munshi Ram Manohar Lal.

Syed, M. H., Akhtar, S. S., & Usmani, B. D. (2011). Concise history of Islam. *Vij Books India Pvt Ltd.*

Tabatabai, M. H. (2010). Bidayah al-Hikmah. *Qom: Jami'ah al-Mudarrisin,.*

Vivekananda, S. (1902). Vedanta Philosophy: Lectures by the Swami Vivekananda on Jnana Yoga. Vedânta Society.

Vivekananda, S. (2019). Complete Works of Swami Vivekananda. *Partha Sinha.*

White, D. G. (2019). *The yoga sutra of Patanjali: A biography*. Princeton University Press.

Yogananda, P. (1952). *Sayings of Paramahamsa Yogananda*. Self-Realization Fellowship Publishers.

Yogananda, P. (1982). *Man's eternal quest*. Self-Realization Fellowship Publishers.

Yogananda, P. (1983). *Songs of the Soul*. Prabhat Prakashan.

Yogananda, P. (2005). *Autobiography of a Yogi: The Original 1946 Edition plus Bonus Material*. Crystal Clarity Publishers.

Yogananda, P. (2008). *Whispers from eternity*. Crystal Clarity Publishers.

Yogananda, P. (2016). *The science of religion*. Ravenio Books.

Zaehner, R. C. (2016). Hindu and Muslim mysticism. Bloomsbury Publishing.

ابن حیون مغربی، نعمان بن محمد، دعائم الإسلام، محقق، مصحح، فیضی، آصف، ج 2، ص 15، قم، مؤسسة آل البیت(ع)، چاپ دوم، 1385ق.

ابوطالبی. (2013). نظریه ی «تکامل جامعه و تاریخ» استاد مرتضی مطهری. معرفت فرهنگی اجتماعی, 15(4), 75-92.

توکلی. (2015). مکتب رامه کرشنه: پیشگام نوزایی دینی در آئین هندو. فصلنامه مطالعات شبه قاره, 7(22), 7-24.

مجلسی، محمدباقر، بحارالانوار، چاپ بیروت، ج ۷۴، ص ۳۰۲، حدیث ۴.

www.ingramcontent.com/pod-product-compliance
Ingram Content Group UK Ltd.
Pitfield, Milton Keynes, MK11 3LW, UK
UKHW022016190726
13853UKWH00005B/1972

9 798886 848779